Poetry Ireland Review 72

Eagarthóir / Editor   **Maurice Harmon**

© Copyright Poetry Ireland Ltd. 2002

Poetry Ireland Ltd./Éigse Éireann Teo. gratefully acknowledges the assistance of The Arts Council/An Chomhairle Ealaíon, the Arts Council of Northern Ireland, and FÁS.

Patrons of Poetry Ireland/Éigse Éireann

Grogan's Castle Lounge
Dr. G. Rosenstock
Eastern Washington University
Fearon, O'Neill, Rooney
Daig Quinn
Twomey Steo Ltd.
Kevin Connolly
Neville Keery
The Irish-American Poetry Society

Desmond Windle
Joan & Joe McBreen
Dillon Murphy & Co.
Office Of Public Works
Richard Murphy
Occidental Tourist Ltd.
Winding Stair Bookshop
Doirín Meagher
Swan Training Institute

Poetry Ireland warmly invites individuals, cultural groups and commercial organisations to become Patrons. Patrons are entitled to reclaim tax at their highest rate for all donations of between €128.00 and €12,700. For more details please contact the Director, at Bermingham Tower, Dublin Castle, Dublin 2, Ireland or phone 01 6714632 or e-mail: management@poetryireland.ie

Poetry Ireland Review is published quarterly by Poetry Ireland Ltd. The Editor enjoys complete autonomy in the choice of material published. The contents of this publication should not be taken to reflect either the views or the policy of the publishers.

ISSN: 0332-2998
ISBN: 1-902121-10-4

Editorial Assistant/Typesetting: Paul Lenehan & Adam Rudden

Cover Design: Colm Ó Cannain
Typography: Barry Hannigan
Cover Photo: Oisín Kelly's 'The Children of Lir', The Garden of Remembrance, Parnell Square, Dublin 1. (Photo courtesy of Mark Granier).

Printed in Ireland by ColourBooks Ltd., Baldoyle Industrial Estate, Dublin 13.

Contents Poetry Ireland Review 72

	3	Editorial
Eamon Grennan/Rachel Kitzinger	5	Colonus Chorus
Eamon Grennan	7	Stepping Out
	7	Storm Poem
Gerald Dawe	8	The Middle of England
	8	The Interface
	9	An Encounter
	9	Love poem
	10	Siesta
James J. McAuley	**11**	**The Drum-Rolls of Doom**
Hugh McFadden	15	Travelling with Patrick Kavanagh (c. 1966)
Eamonn Wall	16	An Incident in Courtown
John Fuller	18	Three for Prue
Ted Deppe	21	Marisol
John McAuliffe	**23**	**Austin Clarke: Three Poems**
Ivy Bannister	26	Earthquake at Yokohama...
Mark Leeney	27	Freedom
Conall Quinn	27	Silver Whales
Rosemarie Rowley	28	stanzas 12-18 from 'Betrayal into Origin'
Ann Leahy	30	Forged
Michael Coady	31	Angels and Ministers of Grace
David Woelfel	34	Tourist
	35	The wrestler Onogawa and the tea-house waitress Ohisa
Joseph Fagan	36	Corncrake
Fred Johnston	36	Absolutes
Hamish Ironside	37	Full Moon
	37	Black Candle
	37	Some Vague Thing
	38	Him and Her
Maria Hoey	39	Alcoholic
Gerry Murphy	40	Further Out
Gerry Hull	41	Lurching Windward
John Hughes	41	Saving the Union
Geraldine Mills	42	This Was No Passover
	42	And I The Hidden
John O'Donnell	43	Missing Persons
Gréagóir Ó Dúill	44	Darkness Falls
Patrick Moran	45	Angler
Todd Hearon	46	Nocturne
	47	Pilgrimage
Padraig Rooney	48	The River at Mohács
	49	Freak
David Butler	49	Glassblower
Joseph Sendry	**50**	**No Room For Wasted Effort**
Tony Curtis	53	The Olympians
	56	Snowlines
Ita O'Donovan	58	Impressions
John W. Sexton	59	my secret witch

Colette Nic Aodha	60	Speaking Minority Languages
Sabine Wichert	61	Of Dreams and Nightmares
Billy Collins	62	Knife and Fork
	63	Evening
	64	The Horn
Ben Howard	65	Nameless
	66	Jack and Jill
	67	Ducked
Eugene O'Connell	68	The Colour of Dereliction
Wendy Mooney	69	Miss Delicious
John McKernan	70	Dear Saint Anorexia
Edward Power	71	Grandfather's Egg
Peggy O'Brien	72	The Oracle
Mike Casey	75	A Splinter Of Light
	76	Geologists
Angela Bourke	77	**Parallel Resources**
Michael Massey	80	Kate At Two
Eibhlín Nic Eochaidh	81	What she remembers now
	81	Incommunicado
	82	Before I left
Declan Collinge	83	Tine Gheimhridh
	83	Winter Fire
Matthew Fluharty	84	Late winter notes
Gerard Smyth	85	Hoard
	85	Van Gogh
Robert Greacen	86	Lord Kelly
William Oxley	87	The Alchemy of Making
	87	Colour To The Town
Janice Fitzpatrick-Simmons	88	The Long Way Home
	89	Taking Names
	89	Bones
John Sewell	90	Carnality / Five Beech Leaves
Harry Clifton	91	To My Wife
	92	North Great Georges Street
	94	Hereafter
Tom Halpin	95	**The Obstinate Quest**
Mary O'Donnell	99	Necessities
	99	Holy
	100	Field Work
Máiríde Woods	101	The Magic Tablecloth
Fred Johnston	102	**Syllables on a White Wall**
Tom MacIntyre	106	Le Premier Fauve
Brian Donnelly	109	**Making It New**
Peter Kane Dufault	113	Scenario
Denis Collins	114	The Parcel
Merrily Harpur	115	The Lesson
Caroline Lynch	116	My Grandfather
Leanne O'Sullivan	117	Crescendo
Noel Monahan	118	The Funeral Game
	119	**Notes on Contributors**
	124	**Books Received**

Editorial/Eagarfhocal

> Who will go drive with Fergus now,
> And pierce the deep wood's woven shade,
> And dance upon the level shore?
> –'Who Goes With Fergus', W.B. Yeats

"Poetry," Thomas Kinsella once wrote, "is an investigation by concerned beings of the vital processes of their lives in youth, in maturity, in happiness, in misery, in old age...poetry can be, for poet and reader, the most serious, intimate and useful thing in the world." That investigation, as Tom Halpin's review of Kinsella's *Collected Poems* makes clear, has continued throughout his career, as has that view of poetry as a serious, rewarding and necessary activity.

In its own way *Poetry Ireland Review* participates in this activity, making itself available to poets who examine and give imaginative expression to experience. In this issue we have poems that focus on a variety of experience at different stages of individual lives, and do so in a serious manner. The editor tries to find some balance among the various topics and styles. But central to what we do is the shared conviction that it is important.

After four issues we see it can be done. It is possible to provide poetry of a high order consistently. Poets continue to send in material on the understanding that the aim is to publish the best and to ensure that we can be proud of the result. *PIR*, as I said initially, is only as good or as challenging, as profound, or as innovative as the poets make it.

There is also the sharing. There is a core of poetry-readers, many of them subscribers, who attend to what is going on, who delight in a new publication by Eiléan Ní Chuilleanáin, or a first collection by Tom French or Mark Granier, to name just three who have recently appeared, or who notice when Geraldine Mills brings out a booklet of promising poems.

There is always room for play – Iggy McGovern and Vincent Woods in the last issue, Michael Coady and Tony Curtis in this. Coady's poem is an example of the imagination transcending pain, running freely, "taking on" the Vatican along the way and at the same time commemorating those who attended him in hospital. The Curtis poem begins lightheartedly in the metaphor of poets taking part in a race, portraying each of the contestants, then turns into a magical evocation of the poetic imagination and concludes with an elegiac reflection on how the race may end.

PIR provides standards and models. In the last issue it seemed to me we had work as good as any being written. It was a delight to discover Eric Ormsby whom I had known for his scholarship, not for his poetry. And there were other significant figures, other examples of fine poetry. *PIR* may also note when a poet changes style, as Aidan Mathews and John Ennis did in the last issue, as Mary O'Donnell and Eamon Grennan do in this. In the case of John Ennis I decided not to use poems I had intended to publish so that we could focus on the elegy, 'Miriam'. In this issue we mark the transition in the work of Gréagóir Ó Dúill to writing in English; he moves without loss of quality from one language to the other. Appropriately, Angela Bourke provides a critical comment on his *Rogha Dánta*.

We learn from one another. Eamon Grennan, who has already caused us to think in his collection of essays, *Facing the Music*, calls attention to what he is doing as a poet. He wants "to step out of shelter to see what I see in the free air, and say it". The poem, he says, "though not all things to all men, should have many things in it", and then proceeds to chisel images into our minds. It is a declaration of intent, bravely made and backed up with evidence. And this, I suggest, is the right place to say it.

Our cover suggests Spring, the flight of the imagination, the connections we make with myth and the lasting fruitfulness of tradition:

> Where wings have memory of wings, and all
> That comes of the best knit to the best...
> – 'Upon a House Shaken by the Land Agitation', W.B. Yeats

translated by Eamon Grennan and Rachel Kitzinger

Colonus Chorus
from Sophocles' *Oedipus at Colunus*

Earth's best dwelling places these
in a land that's rich in horses —
here you have arrived stranger
in bright shining white Colonus.
Here the sweet-voiced nightingale
    throngs with song
glades untouched by wind and sun.
The wine-flecked ivy grows in these
thick untrodden groves of the god.
    And you'll find
    fruits in plenty
unbitten by the breath of winter.
Here with his divine attendants
roams the Bacchic Dionysus!

Here beneath the dew of the sky
the narcissus never withers –
forever weaving an ancient garland
for the brows of the two great goddesses.
And here – behold! – the golden crocus.
The streams unsleeping never empty
spreading from the wide Cephisus.
    Ever running never dry
day by day this pure water
floods the plain and keeps on quickening
mile after fertile mile of earth.
Even the Muses don't shun this place –
    nor even she
with her golden reins: Aphrodite!

And here is something I've never heard of
growing in the fields of Asia
nor the far-famed Doric isle of Pelops:
a tree that seeds itself by nature!
Self-created
sacred even
to the weapons of our enemies!
Here the grey-leafed olive flourishes:
nourisher of children.
No young man nor old man either
can lay a fatal hand on it
for ever-waking Zeus protects it
– patron of the sacred olive –
and his grey-eyed child Athena!

And here is one more word of praise
I'll offer to our mother city!
It's the country's proudest boast
given by the god himself –
god of horses colts and shining ocean!
Son of Kronos Lord Poseidon!
It was you
who raised the city with this gift –
so we boast of it today.
You who gave the bridled harness
healing horses of their wildness
and on these pathways first transformed them.
And you gave another wonder:
Oar-blades to tame the waves
and gallop flashing in the wake
of the hundred-footed Nereids dancing!

Eamon Grennan

Stepping Out

Now that the buried stones have risen to earth's surface and would almost
Talk to me; now that the tall hawthorn by the gate keeps making its snaggy
Passes at me when I walk out under a dome of shouldered hay; now that
The nimble blood has dried under the mud caked on my knuckles, leaving
Two small crimson badges signifying nothing except the fact I can't handle
A sickle the way my neighbour can, who slices back fuchsia bush and briar
To a neat avenue of clean-cut branches; and now that the bees have come
Back to take over the dark world above my head again, where they lead
Their incessant, endangered, singleminded lives, boiling in the attic – isn't it
Time to step out of shelter to see what I see in the free air, and say it?

Storm Poem

Skelped, ice-bladed, fairly scarified by this gale with hail in its teeth,
I keep seeing the rainbow in the belly of the storm and go on thinking
The poem, though not all things to all men, should have many things in it:
The gale, the hail, the rainbow, the way these ice grains hop off the grass
And how your cheek feels, being struck, not to mention that dark-headed
Scuttling plover, the yolk-yellow flowers of furze that signal salvation
To this grey February air, or the stream so high over its stone causeway
It can't be crossed and I have to consider my few options and turn back
The way I came and (turning the other cheek to hailstone and wind-nip)
Learn what *storm of circumstance* really means, and *winds of change*.

Gerald Dawe

The Middle of England

I don't know what possessed me
Sitting in the kitchen one overcast
August day, listening to cricket
On the radio. It's overcast there, too,

In the middle of England,
As a car alarm beeps away.
But the commentary is hypnotic
Though what it all means

I have to imagine,
Through the covers, deep square
On the boundaries, we're told
They anticipate rain.

The Interface

'The lights are going on in towns that no longer exist'
and in the districts we never knew we lived in
between the cemetery where turncoat rebels
are reputedly buried and the narrow road north.
In the parlours of the very few who stayed put
The Telegraph's folded, the curtains in perfect order
and the radio putters in the background. Good news
is rarely expected – the kids are well grown and gone
to Scotland, Canada, the West Country, and for all
the time they spent together little remains the same:
£ shops and discount bars and fast food joints
and even the church is up for sale.
*See. What did I tell you. It is the case
that the biggest fall is the fall from grace.*

Gerald Dawe

An Encounter

I purloined this one from Ron –

Walking the dog one afternoon
He spots at the lakeshore
An old Vietnamese woman fishing,
Her bicycle left by a tree.

This, however, is Switzerland.

She is at the delta of a river
That goes on forever where her
Village sits at the back of her mind
And the silence she hears

Is of a completely different kind

To the hushed busyness of this
Place which she's made her own,
Changing all before her in
The time it takes to catch a fish.

Love poem

I hear her shower, the water spills.
She moves, draws the curtain rail, towels,
Her feet pad about in the smallest room,
Life and soul, all of her, overhead; unseen.
*

Haunch, thigh, hip, jaw line –
Like a Buddha before me.
Breast plate, shoulder blade,
Your lips in flight confirm.
*

The amber streetlight's still ablaze
But you are miles and miles away –
Only cliff face and the empty beach
As far as the eye can see.

Gerald Dawe

Siesta

They are moving the furniture about
In hell. Around this time each day
The scraping and shifting begins.

Or else, in the ever so bright afternoon,
The idiot kid makes sure we all hear
The western or soap opera that blares
Out over the de Chirico street.

Even as I speak the dark rooms
Are filled with the dubbed action films
We may as well all be watching.

Leave it to me, he seems to be saying,
When you awaken from your slumbers,
I will recall the human world
You thought you had escaped.

James J. McAuley

The Drum-Rolls of Doom

John F. Deane, *The Hero, Home*, Icarus Editions No. 4, The Dedalus Press, pb €7.50.
Mark Granier, *Airborne*, Salmon Poetry, pb €8.88.
Nigel McLoughlin, *At The Waters' Clearing*, Flambard/Black Mountain, pb €11.50.
Joseph Woods, *Sailing to Hokkaido*, Worple Press, pb €£9.50.

The Hero, Home is the fourth in John F. Deane's Icarus Editions pamphlets, encompassing an ongoing series of poems which make a significant contemporary contribution to our long tradition of devotional/mystical poetry, stretching back through Denis Devlin and Thomas MacGreevy to A.E., thence to Mícheál Óg Ó Longáin and the Bardic tradition, all the way to St. Colmcille, anonymous scribal verses, St. Patrick's Breastplate, etc. His poetry is all the more necessary when there are no longer ecclesiastical patrons to commission them, nor tightly-knit religious communities to receive them. Also, of necessity, Mr. Deane's poems are radical departures from the pietisms of his Victorian and modernist predecessors.

In this pamphlet, he brings together his "readings" and "versions" of the Anglo-Saxon and medieval poems which were seminal in the development of his spiritual and aesthetic consciousness: 'The Dream of the Rood', 'The Seafarer', and 'Father to Son', from a Latin poem of St. Colman. He adds two original poems, 'Knock' and 'From a Far Country'. The latter harkens back to the persistent themes of earlier poems in his Icarus series, though considerably more serene compared to 'Far Country', the title poem of Icarus No.1. Icarus No. 3, *Upon Foreign Soil*, also carried forward the motif of the spiritual condition as exile in a strange – though not always unpleasant – place. His introduction usefully explains the origins of his interest in the "strange worlds" of Anglo-Saxon literature, as they "echo my own experiences, for I was born where seas are rough and lives are tossed and tumbled at the mercy of those seas."

There are moments, isolated phrases perhaps, which can easily be taken out of the tapestry that Mr. Deane has woven for them and found humourous or even farcical. Nevertheless, the reader who shares, however hesitantly, the spirit in which he has composed them will be amply rewarded.

It's a surprise to find that *Airborne* is Mark Granier's first collection, for he's left his signature on the poets' attendance sheets, here and in Britain, "for over two decades", the jacket informs us. His poems are typically brief, epigrammatic like 'A Show Of Hands', or imagistic in the W.C. Williams manner, like 'Portrait Sketch', or the exit-poem, 'Vanishing Point'. Hence the book seems slight for two decades' work. Only one poem, 'Tree-Diving', a boyhood memoir in ten quatrains, requires a second page.

Mr. Granier's craft relies on the precision of his diction, for he leaves himself very little room to convey "increments of meaning" through figuration or prosodic devices. That he succeeds so admirably in so many of these poems is testimony to his wit and flair for puns, chiselled descriptive phrases, and skilfully veiled metaphysical undercurrents. Here's 'Advice To Adolescents':

> Rave to the slackly made and woefully sung
> (the worse the better); be moody, unstrung
>
> for days, in love with the drum-rolls of doom.
> *Never* tidy your room.

'Ancient View Of Amsterdam', on a Rembrandt etching, opens with a pun, "A skyline accumulates from scratch", and closes nine lines later with:

> …a windmill, and further off
>
> in the dismantling haze,
> three others, lighter and lighter,
>
> cartwheeling across the horizon.

There is a touching elegy for the Diceman, and a mock-apocalyptic poem about being awakened by a vacuum cleaner, and several more of such quality as to have Mr. Granier shadowing the likes of Louis MacNeice, W.R. Rodgers, and Eamon Grennan, who writes a commendation for the jacket.

Nigel McLoughlin is a credit to the talent-spotting powers of the late James Simmons, and Janice Fitzpatrick-Simmons, who continues to keep the hospitable doors of the Poet's House open in Falcarragh, Co. Donegal. Mr. McLoughlin has recently completed his Master's degree there; this first collection bears witness to his originality and the fibrous timbre of his diction, as well as his struggles with the degree's requirements. There is an 'Anti-Sestina', the irregular lines fulfilling, more-or-less, what the late Robin Skelton termed the "obsessive" rolling repetition of the end-words. There are three stiff translations from the Irish, a John Berryman imitation, a couple of unrhymed sonnets (I think), some forays into what Robert Frost termed the "tight iambic", and a short prose-poem – all accomplished with almost stony aplomb. His best work is in the "loose iambic" cadences redolent of his Ulster region, Enniskillen and the Lough Erne hinterland.

The central poem, 'Lines', offers us nine brief scenarios from the world of the eel-fishermen of the Lough. The tone is subdued, the details resonant, the ramifications of the extended metaphor well controlled:

> These days I run my lines by metre
> Not the yard, but still I circle,
> Box them in and check the hooks.
> I run them shore to shore, have pushed
> Apart the weight, the float and set
> My lines to fish the deeper water.

Similarly striking are 'Quarterlights', four "views" from local places, and the two final poems, 'Belfast' with its restrained elegiac cadence, and 'Stones', with its carefully modulated satire:

> Our dead rhetoric returns,
> In sentences, parsed with guns.
> It echoes off walls…

His short love-lyrics are weakened by slack rhythms and trite phrases; but then the very best poets have written flawed love-poems, as documented by Wyndham Lewis and Charles Lee in *The Stuffed Owl*.

The sensations, observations, and sometimes elliptical associations rendered by a poet with the whole planet in his hip-pocket make for entertaining, insightful reading in this first book from Joseph Woods, also an alumnus of the Poet's House. He captures atmosphere, rather than a deeper sense of place, travelling on the trans-Siberia express or aboard the

Hokkaido ferry of the title. For the most part he uses spare, imagistic forms which bring the isolated sights, sounds and movements into momentary stasis, rendered with varying degrees of precision. 'Salvaging a Sweetness' uses this technique shrewdly, running just two sentences through thirty-three accentual hemistichs for a dramatically successful to-and-fro effect.

These are likeable, open-handed poems, inviting us into the poet's experiences – both as foreign journeys and as explorations of language and verse techniques. Only when he seems uneasy himself do the poems lose momentum or fail to find a resolution. He seems more assured when he allows himself to be expansive, as in the book's last three poems. In 'Mrs. Moon', the narrator sits enjoying the vista from the stoop of an old couple's home,

> ...lost in the negative space
> of some vast woodblock print. Moonlight files a glint
>
> over water held in an ancient field. Laughter comes
> from the kitchen, old man's wife and you. We've come
> through, we've come through...

He and his companion will continue their journey the next day:

> ...and there being no paths,
> we'll walk the walls, lured by the sound of falling water,
> to bathe in the bottomless blue they talk about.

Acceptance closes a poem that has dramatised the traveller's restive need to move on, even from tranquil scenes. 'Cagayan de Oro' centres on a group of boys diving for coins thrown by the passengers from their ship, but refuses the easy resolution, leaving the narrator morally stymied. 'Landship' is the kind of work-poem (mechanised potato harvest) I'm most partial to, the rhythms enacting the dogged tedium, the details building unobtrusively to the curiously contradictory epiphany:

> ...I have found my pitch
> in this season of evictions.
> A place on a moving belt above earth
> with a part scraping it.

Hugh McFadden

Travelling with Patrick Kavanagh (c. 1966)

There are some moments that live on
in my memory, some images
that remain and shine in the sun
after the fog of morning lifts.

Such a moment comes to mind as
when I saw you, Patrick Kavanagh,
sitting upstairs on the 12 bus,
Panama-style boater perched on head
pushed back jauntily from forehead,
as you silently gazed at the scene:
mid-morning on Upper Leeson Street
heading for the canal bridge and town,
the sun shining down on saint and sinner.
You had recently returned from the States,
hence the straw hat, the air of a stranger;
no, a lover returned to his beloved
City of God incarnate in the world
in the commonplace streets of Dublin.
Passing over the bridge on the canal
we then travelled near the realm of heaven.

Eamonn Wall

An Incident in Courtown

When they want to know on Judgement Day
what I've done to save the world from
doom, I'll say one summer afternoon I sat at a
window table of Joe's Café in Courtown
mindful of Sarah Connolly from Dublin 4.
I was drinking through a straw from a bottle
of Bubble Up, awaiting my selected song to
sound from the juke-box after the Philistine
minds and filthy coppers had had their fill
of Cliff Richard & Petula Clark. My sole
selection 'Don't Let Me Down', three
plays for a shilling. Well worth the wait.

Below in the harbour an old man on a brown
chair applied tar to his boat, thinking himself
a model county Errol Flynn or Francis
Chichester, as along the strand waves and
bathers reclined, the water glistening as once
was its wont on those August days. Above
the café on combed grass Sarah Connolly
putted with Foxrock Nick FitzGerald. He
was helping her with her stroke. They had
crossed hand-in-hand by the cliff walk from
Ardamine, then paraded Gatsby-like under
the café windows & across my line of sight.

Each summer, Joe and his wife returned
quietly from England to dust & air & open
for the season. They were Ramseys come
through long years of peacetime, rowed to
one quiet hill above the harbour lights on
slow July nights. The floors swept, shelves
stocked, & change counted. Hold hands,
kind lovers, count the cars, stop the clocks.
How brief our time of walking. How quickly
as we bother water cools & autumn settles.

Two more shillings in the juke-box, six more
'Don't Let Me Downs', lovers from South
Dublin entering for number four. I caught my
breath, she tugged her skirt on sitting down.
Foxrock Nick ordered two coffees & cream.
Fair-haired goddess in a North Wexford café,
elbows on formica, she knew the ways of post-
céilí roads, I suspected. Forget the moon, look
at those eyes chilled by blue waters of the bay.

On number 5, Joe plugged out the juke-box,
8 'Don't Let Me Downs' too heavy for a
gentle sensibility honed over time in Bradford
or Crewe on Vera Lynn, weak cups of Tetley's
tea. Son, I know your game. Time to go home.
His smile so gentle & discreet no hope of an
international incident. Barred for a time from
Joe's Café for insistence and infatuation, then
walking into the blind wonder of that afternoon,
the likes of which have passed from the world,
headed for the carnival like Updike's young
loser in his story, just pink-slipped by the A&P.

What stirs now in Joe's Café? How much can
light catch of ripped-up tile? What airs sound
on discarded hinges, on woodwork swollen by
the sea? For those who have bred their own,
this plateful of blue water will not recoil from
limestone, marl, sand, lightship & the storms
that have moved across the frame. Observe
again from the wooden bridge by the golf links
how a river halted by sand can never meet the
sea but must retreat like memory to the old
harbour. She was a great beauty & he was a
quiet listener, if truth were ever to be revealed.

John Fuller

Three for Prue

1. *A Boy Writing*

This solemn shrimp, poring over his slate,
Is as naked as the hope he embodies.

One knee is lifted to support the careful capitals,
As if he is ready to leap up from his stool in joy.

But for the moment he is caught in alabaster,
In a lucidity of concentration.

Writing gets no more serious than this,
The first slow act, the letters about to shout aloud.

And you, my dearest, who have the knowledge
At the very heart of you, often near breaking it,

You must know that this little putto has a meaning
For you alone, for all you have achieved

For children whose similar beauty is only damaged
By the slightest crack in the smoothness of the marble

And whose own exclamations of gratitude and joy
Are as eternal as sculpture, and as silent.

2. *Two Kites*

Yours is a ruffled red bird,
Mine a staring green eye and a tail.

You ride the wind and sing,
I sidle and weave.

Where did we come from
Before we went aloft, adventuring?

We had been cared for by a few who had known
The simpler energies of horses and candles.

Is this why we search for such elemental things?
Here we are; and there we were.

The world's a wild place.
We reach out as we can.

Weak struts, papery ribbons, a drum of thread,
And the hope of an afternoon of air.

The strings hum, unreeled from the chest.
When they cross, it is mine that snaps

Who cares who goes first, the sky so blue?
It is the humming, and the tug.

Your kite is steady above us.
Its flying shadow darkens the field.

The grass flickers at its passing.
The grass darkens and burns.

3. *Primroses*

An anonymous archangel called in to say
That the primroses we picked will last another day.

How many times have we bunched the stems,
Cradling the heads in a single leaf of their kind?

How many such small crowds of flowers
Have looked over their green glazed rim

As if to wonder what sort of a space they were in,
Blankly, as their yellow pales into cream

And the green at the centre is a forgotten dream,
An echo of that cold season before growing?

You who have been called to a great exploit of rescue,
To raise the flower on its broken stem

Know that this business of caring is the need
To restore an elemental touch.

These are like all your assisted children,
Who would certainly crowd if they could

With a similar reach and twist of the head
To smile their sweetest smiles for you.

Gathered by you along the winding hedges of your life,
Noticed particularly in their own shorter journey.

Sweetness out of ditches, cardigan smells,
Granny's smell, Edie's smell, the sweetness of memory.

Sweetness in your loose fist, the sweetness
Of following you down this ancient lane for ever.

Ted Deppe

Marisol

When I quit my nursing job
    I stepped out into summer stars
        and clicked my heels in the air.

    Did Dante feel guilty
as he left the Inferno? – all those voices calling
        remember us to the living –

        Security cameras
    caught my leap
        and the supervisor

        froze the frame all night
    so day shift could see
        that look of pure joy.

I left the psych unit to write in Ireland. Marisol
    had just returned.

    I can be watching the island children
        run down the pier, back from their field trip
        to the mainland,

        or a hooded crow
    might drop a mollusk on the rocks
        to crack its shell, and –

Her pale, dirty face framed
    by matted black hair.
    Some keenness behind those dark eyes
        as if she'd been raised
    by wolves.

    She'd stabbed her foster father
with a pencil, her fourth failed placement –
    beautiful Marisol

who'd first come to our children's unit
when she was five – something broken
   behind those eyes, and fierce –

she'd bit off the head of a parakeet.

At the seawall, the island children call
   to the spring tide to swell up
     and pelt them
       with rocks and spray.

They shriek,
     cover their heads and run,
then return laughing to the slipway
   and taunt the sea again.

          And the children
   in the hospital courtyard?
Those who will call out
   to anyone beyond the high, link fence?

Marisol walks on stilts
   through the garden
     and won't look at her birthmother
who's finally come to visit.

She plants one leg down and
   swings her hip into
     the next step, striding

through the blaze
   of sunflowers:
     her mother and that nurse

   can go to hell while this dance
     is played out,
       back straight, head high,
     everyone calling.

John McAuliffe

Austin Clarke: Three Poems

In June 1915 the Jesuit journal *Studies* published an intriguing essay by Prof. George O'Neill on "assisted verse-making", the subject of an experimental class that he had been teaching at Earlsfort Terrace. In the essay, 'Students as Verse-makers', he describes how he set his students the task of versifying specific prose extracts (by William Hazlitt, Philip Sidney and Plutarch, among others) and imitating certain forms and styles. O'Neill's class may well be the first example of a university creative writing workshop: its aim was to uncover new poets and to otherwise stimulate students' understanding of how poetry works. But the essay's interest is not confined to its prescient discussion of poetry workshops: one of O'Neill's students would be a dominant voice in Irish poetry for the next sixty years.

O'Neill notes in particular this student's skill, whose initials he gives as A.C., and he quotes, as examples of his class's success, three of his efforts. The university calendar for that year shows the only B.A. student with those initials is Austin Clarke, then nineteen years old, and indeed the poems' grand vocabulary and their mixture of Yeatsian and gothic touches are also identifiable as trademarks of the poet who would in 1917 make an acclaimed debut with *The Vengeance of Fionn*. Below are O'Neill's set prose extracts and Clarke's apprentice versions of those extracts, the first in quatrains, the second in a Spenserian stanza, the third in blank verse.

1) *"There is a place called "The Valley of the Rocks", bedded among precipices overhanging the sea, with rocky caverns beneath, into which the waves dash, and where the seagull for ever wheels its screaming flight. On the top of these are huge stones thrown transverse, as if an earthquake had tossed them these, and behind there is a fretwork of perpendicular rocks, something like the Giant's Causeway."*
 –From Hazlitt's 'My First Acquaintance with Poets'

    Ah love! there is a little lonely valley
        Beside the summer sea;
    Red flowers and speckled rocks fantastically
        Peep out thro' greenery;

There is a cirque of slender pillars, rooted
        In stately row on row,
That haply grew to magic music luted
        By Orpheus long ago.

All day the sapphire waves are gaily dancing
        A fairy rigadoon;
While high above the seagulls, brightly glancing,
        Laze thro' the purple noon.

And o'er the vale a wondrous Peace by sunlight
        Doth shine in heaven's blue,
And silently by starlight and by moonlight
        It cometh with the dew.

Ask not where is that little lonely valley
        I know not if it be.
I made it in sweet dreams fantastically,
        Ah, Love! for you and me.

2) *"It was even twilight when he entered the city of Antium, and many people met him on the streets but no man knew him. So he went directly to Tullus Aufidius's house, and when he came thither he got him up straight to the chimney hearth, and sate him down, and spake not a word to any man, his face all muffled over. They of the house, spying him wondered what he should be, and yet they durst not bid him rise. For, ill-favouredly muffled and disguised as he was, yet there appeared a certain majesty in his countenance and in his silence: whereupon they went to Tullus, who was at supper, to tell him of the strange disguising of this man."*
        –from Sir Thomas North's translation of Plutarch's *Lives*

    Unhesitant and sure, with soft footfall
    He enter'd thro' the marble portico,
    And in the dazzling brightness of the hall
    Amid the silenced crowd he sat him low,
    Wrapt in his cloak; and no one there might know
    If 'twere some horrid phantom from the tomb,
    Some stricken creature of Plutonian woe,
    Or living man. Then wildly thro' the room
    Strange breathless whispers crept of guiltiness and doom.

A moment only – and some cried aloud
"This is a witless thrall hath wandered here
Unnoticed in our revellings. See! Bowed
And raimented in rags he sits – all fear."
They laughed; yet in the stranger did appear
Somewhat of sad stern majesty exprest,
That silenced every mocking tone and sneer,
Until, halftroubled with a vaguer unrest
And wonderment, they sent for Tullius in haste.

3) *"O, said he, you will never live to my age, without you keep yourself in breath with exercise, and in heart with joyfulness; too much thinking doth consume the spirits; and oft it falls out that while one thinks too much of his doing, he leaves to do the effect of his thinking. Then spared he not to remember how much Arcadia was changed since his youth; activity and good fellowship being nothing in the price it was then held in; but according to the nature of the old-growing world still worse and worse. Then would he tell them stories of such gallants as he had known; and so with pleasant company shortened the way's length."*
                                              –from Sir Philip Sidney's *Arcadia*

All in the golden light of eventime
He gathered them around and spake these words:
"This is the lesson I have won by years
From the tangled truths and fancies of mankind:–
The soul rejoices in the radiance
And proud sweet strength of splendidly-bodied youth,
She blossoms forth in joy and loveliness
Mellowing in the fruitage of old age,
But pent within herself by sickly thought
And too-much scrupling withers up and falls...
"But those of Arcady," he sighed, "love not
The quest of truth or manly deeds as once
When I, now old, was young." And thus he chid
With aged querulous voice his listeners
All in the light of eventime.

Ivy Bannister

Earthquake at Yokohama: September 1, 1923

Remember how the pier rose out of the sea?

Ready to sail, the vast *Empress*
Strained at her anchor.
Small boats darted beneath us.
The shore was a bright print
Of bunting, traders, rickshaw men,
Wharves heaped with merchandise.
On the pier, silken nobles and parasols
Rubbed shoulders with the British.
The hot sun kissed the violet sea,
The air shimmered with prosperity.
Then, a splendid arc, this cambered pillar,
Reached up towards the sun,
A bright vision that hovered
For one pulse only,
Then disintegrated before our eyes.
Granite, earth, people hailed into the sea.
Buildings imploded. Flames
Scoured ruins, scourged the dead,
Blacked the air. Burning oil
Surged down the hillside,
Invaded even the sea.

One perfect moment before the maelstrom.

Mark Leeney

Freedom

Hair done up tight
As a balled fist
Softness roped into strength

If she let it spill free
It would ripple and spread
With the wildness of
Horses' manes
And her heart would be the heart
Of a wild horse of the Camargue
Running unhindered

Conall Quinn

Silver Whales

The great islands steamed
the earth grew hungry.
Trees dying and being born
called two silver whales from the sea
to lay down among the rocks.
When they died they became rocks.

And the sea became a silver whale
and with a tremendous ebony breath
the sea retreated and was gone.

Rosemarie Rowley

stanzas 12-18 from 'Betrayal into Origin (Dancing and Revolution in the 'Sixties)'
Winner of the Scottish Open International Competition, Long Poem Prize 1996

12.
In the dim days when dancing was a sin
Convent girls were taught they mustn't swagger
Or fade to where the walls and hopes were thin
In the era before rock 'n' roll and Mick Jagger
Arguments abounded, and who would win
For women's flowering, when all sought to gag her
Salvation was the only goal, and the distant din
Of wars and rumours made rich the carpetbagger
Whose daughters in the convent school for wives
Had as their daily text cloistered lives

13.
The holy retreat when the priest sermonised to warn
Against the world, the flesh, and the devil
He was among girls he was born to scorn
And his picture of hell showed many a revel
In his fiery rhetoric he mixed with the alien porn
The fright of imagination where he could level
Old charges on the girls, in original sin born
Here innocent for a while, but boys would dishevel
These neat heads, boys who at a dance
Could turn into a fiery devil at a glance

14.
She left school with her honours intact
The boys nearly fainted when they heard
All men had liked to pontificate
Making her dismissed as a brainy bird
Male bonding such a heavy syndicate
An intelligent woman was being too absurd
Her job would be to type his letters in triplicate
And not her own stuff, for such was woman's word
She lost her dream of equality in the office
Making the daytime world powerless and loveless

15.
So, having foresworn the convent as a bourgeois dream
Of advantageous desire or prudent concupiscence
She would have to search for love in a different scheme
And opted then for dancing's munificence
Such was her skill with movement she would redeem
Those days when all was boring competence
In transcribing notes, she'd have independence and esteem
The night-time and a lover's magnificence
True love and companion to be sought in a haze
Of mirrors, powder, and the ballroom craze

16.
In her dream, the shadow and the light
Tireless in motion, like a perpetual star
Twinkling with love, and incandescent, bright
Like the difference between male and female are
With luminous numinous form, each man a sight
Of the deity, as the cosmos each day dances far
Into infinity with the many and the one, right
On a course of complexity, yet on a par
With justice, beauty and salvation
Dancing became her inspiration

17.
This was before the celebrated mini
Before women's lib scored an own goal
She went dancing every night, it was her destiny
Her prayer, her contact with the oversoul
One partner had wet hair, it was stiff and satiny
Could he be the one who asked her to do the stroll?
Another one was tall, another skinny,
As they twisted, then went on to rock 'n' roll
The ballroom was a class and tribal hunt
With conversation like a daring high wire stunt

18.
One had pimples, and bright red curly locks
His face was pasty, yet he was romancing
He had bright button eyes with laugh line shocks
And a motor bike better than any Lansing
He wore check trousers and bright yellow socks
And looked at her as if she were enhancing
His life at week-ends, scrambling over rocks
And with him be daring, be all-chancing
This date was forbidden by her mother
He was dangerous, and not worth the bother

Ann Leahy

Forged
Prize-winner, Moore Literary and Historical Society Award, 1999

A hammer, an anvil, a soldering iron:
these he left along with his name
given to the grandson born
the year he died and to the great-grandson
who will never know either of them.
A name linking them to a chain

of forebears who exist as threads through
scraps of stories. But who knows
what we owe them. A crooked smile? A tilt
of the chin? A stubborn brow that keeps you
struggling on when everyone would let you go?
The past – it inhabits us; we live up to it,

react against it, fill it out like a prescription.
You skit around on gravel until you find
that that's where you've been tethered all along:
outside the back door of the forge.

Michael Coady

Angels and Ministers of Grace
from 'The Place of Hurt and Healing'

I dream that I am arguing in Irish
with the Pope and his confrères
about the ban on women priests.

Mo náire thú, a Phápa,   My shame on you, Pope,
I lash out *go líofa,*   I lash out fluently;
tú féin agus seana-leaids an Chúria   yourself and the old lads of the Curia
ag swanáil timpeall is ag cogar mogar   swanning around and hugger-muggering
in bhúr ngúnaí galánta corcra nó bána   in your fancy gowns of purple or white
faoi shíleáil iontach Mhícheálangelo.   under Michaelangelo's marvellous ceiling.

Brazenly and fluently I make my case,
quoting to the holy fathers
corporeal miracles of our time,
transcending death and gender.

Nach dtuigeann sibh, I rail infallibly,   Don't you understand?
that a priest in mortal need might nowadays
through benefit of after-death donation
be blessed to embrace and embody
a woman's eyes or heart,
kidneys, lungs or liver?

And conversely –
a resurrected woman
could be walking around
or making love while unaware
that her replacement vital organs
were endowed with Holy Orders?

Ar aon nós, leanaim orm go rábach,   In any case, I go on vociferously –
féach an chaoi a bhfuil cúrsaí   see how we're fixed down
anseo i Ward B, Level 3,   here in Ward B, Level 3
i gcathair na long, ar bhruach na Laoi: in the city of ships, on the banks of the Lee.

There's Francesca from Milan
who watches over us all night,
calling out *arrivederci* in the morning

when she's going home
to see her son out to school
and get some sleep.

There's Alma from the Philippines
who checks on my incisions and courteously
inquires about my bowels.
(Once a month or so she gets through
to her husband and her daughter
at the house of an Irish priest
in the middle of the night
on the far side of the world.)

There's Imelda from Graunnabrahar
who does the morning obs
and deftly takes blood samples
though inconsolably in shock since
over-confident Cork hurlers
were dropped-on by Limerick
a week ago at *Páirc Uí Chaoimh*.

There's Geraldine from Cashel of the kings
who remakes beds and shines up floors
and empties all that must be emptied,

along with Sinéad and Marie
from Mitchelstown and Clonakilty
who carry in the meals,

and not forgetting Joan from Sundays Well
who later on will come round corridors and wards
with tinkling bell and veiled ciborium
of *panis angelicus* on special offer.

Éist, a Chearúil ró-ró-naofa,	Listen here, Karol, most most holy
surely no carnally conceived manjack	
of the red-robed college would deny	
an taobh eile de leaba an tsaoil	the other side of the bed of life –
go háirithe ó thárla é bheith	especially since it's
ó dhúchas chomh teolaí?	so naturally cosy?

For isn't it one of the original mysteries
the way God's almighty divilment

saw fit to throw men and women
together in the world
in an eternal entanglement
of mutual mystification and delight,
torment and damnation,
succour and salvation?

These women here, *adeirim*,   I say
and others I could name
are no more *Micheálangelo* angels
than you or me. They're just
as fabulously fallen, but in my book
they need no bishop's benediction
to be what they're already here –

'sé sin le rá,   which is to say,
ina steille beatha,   alive and kicking,
flesh-and-blood
priestesses.

Rome has weathered wild Gaels
from the west before. The old Pope
frowns and throws his eyes up
towards the Last Judgement.

He's stuck for words,
shackled to the *cúpla focal*   basic phrases
drilled in by Ó Fiaich in '79.

Dia dhuit, he fences.   God be with you, he fences.
Dia is Muire duit, I point.   God and Mary with you, I point.
Dia is Muire dhuit is Pádraig, he parries.   God, Mary and Patrick, he parries.
Dia is Muire dhuit is Pádraig agus Bríd –   God and Mary, Patrick and Brigid –

I palpably hit home.

Bíodh sin mar atá.   So let it be.
I've had my say in the Sistine Chapel
and wake up with the secret
satisfaction of a job well done,

the illusion that I've won.

David Woelfel

Tourist

Graffiti on the old city walls, vespa, chattel, eyelid

the postcard of a little black statue. That January
we left something of ourselves everywhere

as if evidence of sensual acts. There was the usual
fare, the fragile things we smashed, your bruised wrist

the half-eaten bags of food. There were empty bottles
though I think I was worse than you. And that

lonely little black statue boy holding a black sword
in the lightness of his hand, and the three or four words

in Italian we learned together one night in the darkness
of a hotel room, words spoken almost exclusively

with the cupola of your mouth. Your possible mouth,
the bent of my tongue, the long clear maps of silence.

Silence. We can add that to the list too. And the slow
careless nature of Tuscan clocks. And the fat fat pigeons.

And sucked-clean oyster shells and the suggestion
of a little black statue boy dropping his weapon each night

and playing in the golden room of an empty museum.

David Woelfel

The wrestler Onogawa and the tea-house waitress Ohisa

Seven p.m., the hour of latticed eyes

when the high tenements on the district's periphery
lean into the sky   find legs   wear cowls of paper sun.

When you could measure the restlessness of a breeze
by the length of its back   crossing the river Toi

to be close to you when all the doors slide open.
Don't tell anyone, but from where I sit I anticipate

these things   your bluest plum skin   a clay eyelid
your belly of dead butterflies, all the hair on your head

combed in a child's tail. The unbound hand
of the calligrapher's wife racing the great cloud of my thigh

sudden as a breeze.

The title of this poem is taken from an 18th century Ukiyo-e print by Shuncho; Ukiyo means "pictures of the floating world"

Joseph Fagan

Corncrake

The corncrake is a lonely
Bird. With his head down,
His "crake crake" is clear
Evidence of a sad existence.

But buried in tall, primitive
Grasses, he finds a kind of happiness,
Elusive to others. Without it,
He is lost; liable to panic; to threat

Of extinction. I listen and identify
Him, here and there, in a long
Meadow. I sense, sometimes, where
He is liable to call next and exult that,

By chance or otherwise, I've got there
Before him. Both of us, mythical and
Lost sources of fathomable courage.

Fred Johnston

Absolutes
for Una Sinnott

Water taking the sky's colour,
Scraped by a chisel of birds –
The insolence of stone in water.

Even the rim of painted houses
Scraping the harbour's text, re-
Stating the boats' declarations.

A girl furtively lovely,
Scrapes of berryful hedge on her
Hands, descends the street of the world.

Hamish Ironside

Full Moon

It's three or so and, as I lie awake,
I know the birds are sleeping that will fly
at his gun's first crack, and the great pines
whose branches will splinter like bone in the birds' stead
at the second crack will spill the poised eggs.

Even sleeping is a game. The full moon
washes a pale strip across his back.
I watch him breathe and fail to quell this envy
of his mastery in the casual trade of gifts
and losses that fill the oblivious day.

Black Candle

As silence stores music: so this black candle, hoarding
light. Outside, the leaves are falling, or snow, or something. Shadows
shiver across the walls with our breath. What numbs our bodies?
Only that old discrepancy as feeling turns to wording.
Rituals lurk among the darkest spots like sleeping lions,
Even in the small sad play between atoms and ions.

Some Vague Thing

A lonely second lost, I pause and guess and turn
To nothing, but the sound of you, my memory,
Retracing solo footprints in the snow, in spring.
A scent persists; my vision mists to mystery
As shadows weave through fallen leaves and voices burn
Like history, smoke like clouds, like some vague thing.

Hamish Ironside

Him and Her

We know now that this was one of those years
between glam and punk, a summer of drought.
But they are oblivious, still wearing hippy
gear, marooned on their tiny island

of shadow. Both are sitting with hands
on kneeling knees and matching home-cut
hair and they look so alike you'd take them
for brother and sister. As we know, they're not.

The difference lies in the looks on their faces.
Hers, bleached by sun, is defiant;
his, shaded, is stifled panic,
as if the camera might indeed

steal his soul. Many years later
with no idea what's happened to her
and no real memory, and no real belief
in the soul, yet not quite disbelief,

he'll think that, given the right conditions
and if we allow such things to exist
the effect of one soul touching another
could be mindless and lasting as light on silver.

Maria Hoey

Alcoholic

When his green fingers had wilted
he sat in the corner of garden he called a suntrap
and eyed the raspberries run to seed
as drunk as he had ever been.

We thought the old dog's dying might shake him
but he merely asked that we bury him in the shade
And when the new pup dined off the ragged gladioli
he mildly conceded that we had a vegetarian on our hands.

We said that he was charmed to grow so warmly old
as though the very air was *Jameson*
Or the wind that skimmed the rotting fence
had borne some poppy magic from the fields.

And when a hoyden autumn wind had stripped the garden bare
our children braided twigs and leaves
throughout his scanty hair
while we, his children, sought to trace
the terrains of another face
and found, aghast, his mellowed age,
had stripped us of our rightful rage.

Gerry Murphy

Further Out

I can't tell you
where this is happening.
I know it's a dream
because the left bank of the Seine
has just appeared directly opposite
the right bank of the Lee.
I know it's daylight
or at least dream daylight,
that silver-grey, residual glow
from some imploding star
shining in your glossy black hair.
I know it's you
because there is not one
even remotely as beautiful
on the stony inner planets
and I know you have been kissing me
for over a minute
because I have just woken up
gasping for breath.

Gerry Hull

Lurching Windward
near Bellarena, Co. Derry

Imagine us lurching seaward to find
a green shelf seventy yards below
lurching windward. Us stopping by a
stone bank neck-high, the compass
spun over the blue to Donegal.

At our feet, there in the middle of
nowhere, two dying wreaths wind-
tattered. What lovers, drunks or crazy
scattered had rushed off the planet,
and to such a fall?

John Hughes

Saving the Union

Cold north wind. Everlasting day almost upon us.
Across Glengall Street dogs scatter in packs of five and six,
As a black dog devours your discarded shadow.

Just as your black tongue touches my black tongue
I desire that you tell me if you spat three times
On the mound of clay you moulded me from.

Strange, your breath smells of neither one of us.
And who is it you wait here so patiently for? Is he one of us?
Tell me so that I can have my death fit and rattle.

Geraldine Mills

This Was No Passover

Somewhere a fulmar gliding, shadows its wing
in this triangle of room. A scrap of window opens out
onto the sky and the wintering of things.
The table at which I write is carved with the burrow of woodworm,
whose tracery of destruction reads like calligrapher's script
and follows along the lines of the wood's own grain.
The smell of poison that rises from the pockmarks
at my writing arm, is that same smell of which my childhood reeked,
how my mother waged war against them all her life,
gave the order to point our gun of death
into the doorways of their homes one by one.
This was no Passover. We picked out their stiff bodies
with the darning needle, before legs buckled on chairs;
beds careened on the beach of lino, dressers leaned,
a dust fine as gold panned upon the floor.

And I The Hidden

Those full versed days, those nights your body
spooned to mine like wild honey made me beautiful.

Even in your sleep you rhymed my eyes,
my thighs, my hair that strayed across your face;
that I believed I was your queen and you my falconer.

Here in this stolen bed the sky tossed with tercel feathers,
you held my face as if it were your precious bird come home

until your wise mouth tasted salt, and you went back
with stardust in your eyes, for all to see
though never guess, it was I who was your lure.

I was your poem when all the lines were mine, the lyric
of your body mine, the stanza missing in between. The hidden.

John O'Donnell

Missing Persons

Such heartbreak in each grainy photograph
the family has tearfully supplied.
What intimacy these blurred moments have,

squinting into holiday sunlight
or laughing in the pub before the dance.
We can almost feel the weight

of what has happened as we glance
and then move on, a little guiltily,
past this inference of absence

that already we well know
we'll never miss, just faces
in the supermarket queue

or waiting at the bus-stop for a bus
in the dusk of urban evening,
so long as it isn't one of us

who disappears without ever really leaving
in between the shadows and the light;
an ending we hardly can believe in

no prayers, no farewells before the flight
and nothing left except these souvenirs:
The cluttered bedroom, eerie quiet

as grim police teams drag the nearby rivers
and comb the undergrowth. Empty chairs.
Clothes in wardrobes, ghosts on hangers.
A hairbrush full of hairs.

Gréagóir Ó Dúill

Darkness Falls

Darkness does not fall:
Light withdraws like youth,
Rain thickens the windows as astigmatism the lens.
Cold fills slowly my marrows' hollow.

The shelves are packed so tight
Slim spines constrict to my fingers' clumsiness.
Bach's B minor mass reminds me that this lingering
Is new, medicine's trojan gift, the skyline faintly visible for too long.

A pale reflexion of my reading lamp
Shows on the window; see we have made a moon,
And counter-tenor sings a sacred part castrate.
The leaves – were glorious – lie littering to mulch.

Spring will come, it always has, they say, kind sun, bird song,
But that is not my business. That view's too long.

Patrick Moran

Angler

Tell-tale signs. Musings. Withdrawals.
That fretted casting and reeling.
Ripples. Unfathomable depths...

When I emerge from my study,
my little daughter lifts her arms,
chanting: *Daddy, Daddy*.

The baby, too, is glad I'm back:
he thumps his toy-strewn table,
his face all elated.

But only you know that I've been
fishing dark waters with my pen.
You scan my eyes for buffetings

and residues; wondering
how far out I've gone, how deep down;
whether I've come up with anything.

    Or nothing.

Todd Hearon

Nocturne
i.m. Adele Dalsimer

   Rain is general,
Adele, over Boston –
calm, ephemeral,
a sound recalling all
  the rain one's known
  the way the poem
recalls the cloud of language
from which its body comes
to which returns.
               Tongues
lie open in the broken
cobbled streets of Boston
catching at the rain
(the gaslamps listen).

Far from your cloud of hurt
lies the open harbour
with its wharves disconsolate
like loves. (A lighthouse answers).

The rain is a poem
falling as it weaves
its broken body home-
ward over (Adele) waves.

Todd Hearon

Pilgrimage

for Rachel Parry, after an exhibition of her work,
'Clothing for the Transformation', Boston, 2000.

Walk on pampooties of fire-
red chilli peppers. Wear

the boa's slough upon
your head, thought's skin.

Assiduous as Daedalus
fix into the wax

crow feathers for your gloves
lined with lizard sleeves.

Mold the mud bowls at your breast
from a gannet's empty nest,

deck with lichen, trim with turf
cooped from local earth. Enough.

Sleep. In the fleece of dreams
the beast to bear you onwards comes.

The ocean knocks. You stand within
birth's portal ready to begin.

Padraig Rooney

The River at Mohács
for Joanna

The gun-metal Danube at Mohács is so still
you wouldn't think the current strong enough
to carry the flat-bottomed ferry across.
It plies from the town to a jetty where a café
with a faded gable advertisement for tyres
guards the reaches. The blue awnings flutter
and a woman at a window shakes a tea towel
before descending to feed a gaggle of geese.
But here it comes, at an angle to the drift
and moored to a taut cable on either bank.
Puttering at water-level signals an engine
and puffs of exhaust disperse downstream
where backwaters meander before the border.
Now it's closer, the ferry's prow lets down
to reveal a tractor and three pre-capitalist cars –
Trabants held together with plastic cement.
The ferryman's helper wears a peaked cap
with a silver anchor. He counts his change.
There's a Hell's Angel long in the tooth,
with a grey ponytail and Davy Crockett jacket,
astride his Harley Davidson, whose sidecar
seats four bobbing cockerels in a wicker cage.
They disembark in the stillness like ghosts,
with a slight smell of diesel and rising dust.
Nothing then for an hour on the gravel slipway.
Only an old man selling onions and plums,
blue ones with the bloom still on them,
turns up and stands straddling his bike.
Near some reeds, schoolboys are swimming
and their larking is almost comprehensible.
Far out the catfish are biting. Across the river
Mohács sleeps in the afternoon heat.
With precise admonitory slaps on the stones
the wake of the ferry reaches us at last.

Padraig Rooney

Freak

Three glider pilots gliding in the Sixties
caught the updraft and were lifted high
above the thermals into the rarefied air
where a thunderstorm tossed them further
in the thin balsaboard that held them up
so that all three baled out with their chutes
drawing them up into the storm's eye,
a freak one, where Thor's thunderclouds
sucked them into a forge of ice smiting
hailstones as big as basketballs at Earth
and wrapped those pilots in cold shrouds
that fell into our atmosphere from chutes
on brittle strings – three giant hailstones
in one of which a pilot still breathed.

David Butler

Glassblower
winner of the LUAS award for Poetry, 2001

It is as though an incandescent swarm
Has clustered, on a spindle of his breath,
To fabricate a hive
In the hot globe of amber.
Or it is as though the air is given hands,
Cupping the molten bubble thrown out
By his steady lung, crafting
The dull red sun until it sets,
Like a premonition of Winter,
Into the fragile geometry of glass.

Joseph Sendry

No Room For Wasted Effort

Richard Murphy, *Collected Poems*, Gallery Press, 2001.

Except for the *The Mirror Wall*, his most recent volume, Richard Murphy's poetry has been unavailable for the last several years. *Collected Poems* now remedies that lack. Comprising work from 1952 to 2000, it enables us to realise the cumulative achievement of this superbly skillful and distinctive poet over half a century. Gauging his achievement involves appreciating his distinctiveness. Unmistakably Irish, Murphy resists further placement into any single, readily available category. For one thing, he has been strenuously ambivalent toward his ascendancy background. In his long historical poem, 'The Battle of Aughrim', all the main characters are on the Irish nationalist side, and if a hero is to be found, it is Patrick Sarsfield. But Murphy claims ancestors on both sides, and he even-handedly questions the ideologies – mainly the theologies – of both, whether espoused in the seventeenth century or the twentieth. Published in 1968, 'Aughrim' implicitly comments on the Vietnam War, another tragic episode in a larger conflict between major powers that shaped the life of a smaller nation. The eerie parallel with events in twenty-first century Afghanistan gives the poem an unexpected contemporaneity, not least as a study in the destructive effects of religious single-mindedness. In Murphy, moreover, the familiar nationalist/cosmopolitan tension in Irish literature takes an unusual form. Though the work for which he is best known ties him to his birthplace in the West and to Connemara, where he lived much of his life, formative influences go well beyond Ireland, including five years infancy and young boyhood in Ceylon, and a succession of schools in wartime England. With the likely exception of 'The Woman of the House', a lovingly remembered elegy for his maternal grandmother, the most vividly imagined poems of his childhood are five situated in tropical Ceylon.

Collected Poems omits a number of previously published works, mostly from Murphy's first and last volumes: *The Archaeology of Love* (1955), which shows him adapting postwar modernist practice, not yet having mastered his own voice, and *The Mirror Wall* (1989), where he demonstrates a vocal mastery so decisive he can ventriloquise through a succession of multifarious personae. *Sailing to an Island* (1963) was his breakthrough volume. Its title poem (also, out of chronological order, the first in *Collected Poems*) relates an excursion that he has recently described as "a rite of passage that changed my life and inspired my poetry."

Resituating himself both physically and poetically on the Connemara Coast, at the fishing village of Cleggan and the outlying islands, Murphy consciously reclaimed his Irish origins. Here, the craft that he plied, whether that of poet or now also of boatman, allowed no room for wasted effort. He made his style precise and economical. This is from 'Sailing to an Island':

> She smothers in spray. We still have a mast;
> The oar makes a boom. I am told to cut
> Cords out of fishing-lines, fasten the jib.
> Ropes lash my cheeks...

He also made the Cleggan environs a stage for life's drama, stripped to elemental extremes. 'The Cleggan Disaster', the long concluding piece in *Sailing to an Island*, evokes, through a succession of details delivered in hammer-like blows, the night-long ordeal of Pat Concannon against a murderous combination of wind and sea that took the lives of twenty-five other fisherman and destroyed the local fishing industry. 'Seals at High Island', which opens the *High Island* volume (1974), pays homage to the persistence of life by describing the imposing – almost ritual – combat and mating of seals, themselves battered by an unrelenting sea.

In the West of Ireland Murphy found abundant remnants from the past, recent or remote, evidence not only of the struggle to survive but also of human effort to lend security and grace to life: among them, beehive-cells and ruined abbeys constructed by medieval monks, stone cottages abandoned by nineteenth-century victims of famine. Murphy's characteristic impulse has been to discover and interpret the meanings hidden in such objects. This impulse culminates in *The Price of Stone*, published in 1985, after he moved to Dublin: the dominant volume from the latter half of his career and the one that, out of chronological order, concludes *Collected Poems*. In this unconventional sequence, he reconfigures the sonnet itself by having products of human making speak to him, each from a specific location and moment in his past. Building readily becomes a master metaphor for the poetic act, and the sonnet sequence an abbreviated life of the poet and commentary on his world. But with a telling difference. The shift in voice structure opens a new direction in interpretation: at the same time that the poet teases meaning from the objects in his world, those objects send back answering judgements of him.

This structural innovation permits Murphy to achieve a layered complexity of feeling – wonder, affection, grief, guilt, disapproval in varying degrees, sometimes exaltation. Simultaneously engaged and removed, his stance in relation to each phase of his life holds in check any gravitational pull toward such excesses as self-pity, sentimentality or rage. In 'Carlow Village Schoolhouse' the site of the building where in famine days his great-grandfather, having turned Protestant, became master and set the family fortunes on an upward course, admonishes him against self-righteousness: "Not forced to sip / The cauldron soup with undying gratitude, / Would *you* have chosen to board a coffin-ship?" The compression of emotion and meaning that he achieves in the sequence shows Murphy at his best. Yet that compression is sometimes – as here – gained at the price of puzzling readers by enigmatic allusions. Few would know, for example, of the existence, much less the significance, of the Carlow Village Schoolhouse. Here the Gallery Press edition can be faulted for providing few explanatory end-notes, and those mainly for 'Aughrim' and 'The God Who Eats Corn'. Wake Forest University Press did much better on this in the American edition. Happily, many obscurities will no doubt be clarified and the autobiographical implications of many poems brought into sharper relief with the forthcoming publication of Murphy's memoir, based on journals kept over a period of years.

A short section devoted to Murphy's most recent work is entitled 'Sri Lanka and Poems of 1989-1992'. His return in the eighties to that island off the Indian subcontinent was quite different from the return in the sixties to those off the Irish coast. During his fifty-year absence, colonial Ceylon had become post-colonial Sri Lanka. In a sonnet ('Where are you going?') that adopts the accusatory, oblique self-address developed in *The Price of Stone*, he finds that a road through a squalid slum "puts on trial your childhood", the childhood recalled in earlier poems with such keen fascination. But the choice product of several return visits to Sri Lanka was not the handful of contemporary reflections on the island nation here collected, but the sixty-two verse renderings of graffiti poems, written in Sinhala from the eighth to the tenth centuries, published as *The Mirror Wall*. Unfortunately, only eight are included in *Collected Poems*. Already commenting on remnants from the past, late fifth-century frescoes of female figures with whom they share a cliffside wall in the interior of the island, the graffiti take Murphy into strange yet somewhat familiar poetic territory. But interpreting these remnants is rather like crossing unbridgeable gulfs – of history, of language, of culture. Murphy's logistical move is to bring play into play, making liberal use of uncertainty itself, mingling his voice in unexpectedly intricate ways with those recorded on the wall. These implicitly deconstructive pieces should prompt us to look again, with sharper focus, at the collected work of this poet who made construction one of his master metaphors. We can expect to be simply delighted with the complexity we discover there.

Tony Curtis

The Olympians

Next up are the poets.
This was never going
to be a glorious race
but, after the pandemonium
of the heats,
let's at least make sure
they're all facing the same way.

Running in lane one
in anonymous and fragments,
with a withered arm
and a halt leg,
it's the Greek beauty Sappho,
all sandy smiles
and dark brown eyes,
it's rumoured
she moves like the wind.

Beside her,
in lane two,
with the haiku –
seventeen steps
of grace and precision –
it's the butterfly
of the short line,
representing Japan,
the little man, Basho.

In three with the sonnet
is William Shakespeare,
his run will depend
on impeccable rhythm,
on getting it all to flow.
Though a shadow is cast
over his selection
with Percy Shelley,
William Wordsworth,

Samuel Coleridge
and George Gordon, Lord Byron
all testing positive for opiates.

In lane four
with the villanelle
its the Welshman Dylan Thomas:
after a lifetime of injuries
and unfulfilled promise –
it's marvellous to see him
finally up on his feet.

In the middle of the field,
standing out like a king,
is the long-distance legend,
blind Homer from Greece.
Kit Smart was a contender, but
he never turned up for the race.

Beside him,
crammed into six,
are Dante –
the Italian wizard,
the antelope of terza rima –
and a couple of farm boys,
Frost and Heaney.
I've seen them in practise,
they move with deceptive ease.

In lane seven, in the four
by four hundred relay,
it's the Russian champions –
they pass the baton
with silk-like grace –
Pasternak to Tsvetayeva
Tsvetayeva to Mandelstam,
Mandelstam to Akhmatova.
She brings it home
with tremendous power
and gritty determination.

Out in lane eight,
going round the bend,

there's an army of poets.
I recognise at least a hundred
faces preparing for the start.

And then,
not with a shot
or a shout,
but with a collective sigh,
they're off.

It is poetry in motion,
like something out of Brueghel
the stillness is absolute,
for no one has moved.

They have closed their eyes
and are imagining
the wind on the face,
the sweat on the brow,
the pain in the chest,
the ache in the heart,
the hardship,
the loneliness,
the grief
that has brought them to this.

Some are already
closing on the line.
Others will take
hours, days, weeks, months.
Some will still be running
when the crowds are gone
when the lights are off
when the stadium's closed.

And some will
never make it home:
their words, their faces,
their lives forgotten.
They will turn to dust
where they fall.
The earth takes back
what it gives away –
the lanes run on forever.

Tony Curtis

Snowlines

Compared to this island
Valentia is a tea cosy,
Spitsbergen a metropolis.

Did you know the word '*Inuit*'
means 'eater of raw meat'?
                          I didn't.

I have been here a year now
and the worst of it is I feel
like St Kevin in the wilderness.

Exhausted sea birds rest for days
when they arrive, closing their eyes
against the bitter north wind.

Grey seals, who love the emptiness,
sing; any time now
I'll be joining in all out of tune:

'*Oh, I'm sailin' away my own true love,*
 I'm sailin' away in the morning'

               *

This is a land that has lost its memory.
Even the hills have forgotten the trees.
Only tufts of grass remember green.
The rest is grey. I stand in the rain,
a wet hood tight around my face,
remembering ash settling on the fire;
smoke flicker as you'd come into the room
naked from a bath, drying your hair
with a towel. I miss your wet footprints
on the wooden floor, the warmth
of your voice, your soft brown eyes.

Sometimes it gets so lonely here
I follow a disused mining track
a mile or two into the hills
to where some poor soul, long
forgotten, has strung a fence
up to the lake and abandoned mines.

It wasn't until it began to snow
that I realised the fence was a guideline
for the old miners back to the jetty
when snowstorms covered the land.

Maybe there's a photograph
on somebody's mantelpiece:
"*Michael by the snowline.
          The winter of '47*"

        *

Every morning I ask myself
'What am I doing here?'
You see, I had planned,
as poets do, to sit by a window
disturbed only by snow
and to make poems
out of the whiteness.
But alone, I lost the need.

Instead, I'm fluent in penguin,
and learning seal songs.
What I've really missed
are not papers or books,
but a settling in my soul.
I've missed you, your garden
and its sway of flowers.

So I've taken fence posts and earth
and made my own garden
at the back of the house.

In the centre of it all,
I've stuck your photograph
in an upturned glass –
the one I took of you in Australia.
Soon I'll have wild thyme
and rock roses coming into bloom.
Already, snowdrops and crocuses
are about to unfurl.

As for the poetry:
this is another plan
that has gone all wrong.

Ita O'Donovan

Impressions

On the horizon, temples of my mind,
a mountain range that is a mandala.
Colours of ivory and almandine
and the soft wind's musk-pear fragrance
brush the sea's surface and quaking sand.
My footprints follow my uncertain dance
until the moon calls time and the tide-wave
scatters grain over them in evening-land.

In morning-land millions of years ago
Lucy left her footprints – not in the snow –
but fossilised in black volcanic ash.
Pollen-tubes spoke of meadows and no trees
for aerial roads – she stood up and walked.
In that leap of imagination Lucy left her imprint.

John W. Sexton

my secret witch

Her grey hair glitters under the moonlight
as she flies above the sea. Whales' fisted heads
part the waves below her. Storms fester
on the tip of her tongue. She seeds the air
with her presence and men turn in their sleep.
She is the nightmare of every child.
Women fear her for they fear they're her.
They're right to think that way. The woman
who falls asleep beside you is part of her dream.
She dreams that she flies above the earth, made
from the dreams of every woman who sleeps.
Sometimes she awakens in a strange place.
A frying pan is in her hand, egg
and sausages sizzling in fat. A child
is screaming in its cot and her husband
is shouting for no reason. Then she's
asleep again, storms festering on her tongue,
the nightmare of every child, every man's
suspicion of who his wife might be.

I know she is there, see her in the shot
of grey of my lover's hair. Await
the day when she stands before me in all
her magnificence, withers me with a single word,
and catching me by the ear
carries me high above the earth.

Colette Nic Aodha

Speaking Minority Languages

It was our first encounter
and our last.
Seeing her helpless shape
I went out of my way to praise,
she startled, shocked I knew her name
or maybe that I read
and spoke a minority language
and if I did
was anyway keen on verse.

Taking her frail hand, I didn't shake it
in case it might break,
amazed that great verse emanates
from such a fragile face
body crooked with age.

Greater *saoi*s spilled out and in
but I rested all my interest with her
until another eager fan took my place.

Yesterday her words froze on her lips
never reaching her fingers.

Sabine Wichert

Of Dreams and Nightmares
for PEB

It was in the seventies that you said,
in this place one has to be married to survive.
I disregarded your advice: I wanted to
open all my possibilities, forget old
dreams of escape and slap every day awake.

Until A. told me that time would heal
what needed healing in her, now that she
felt secure: husband, status, two sons. Her
milk would not curdle, she would never
need to chew and rechew yesterday's grass.

And B. praised his wife, when I asked,
as a perfect mother and good housewife
equal to none. He was all earnest seriousness
as if he wanted me to say well done
and well achieved. I could not take it.

So I took my dream from its shelf and
dreamt it again: the old library full of
women and men pondering the outside's fate
in peace, having tea served silently and
going for walks in the park now and then.

Only sometimes this dream becomes a nightmare
and despite the rain I want to sit and eat and
drink in the night-air at street-cafes, stroll through
the secret back-alleys, prod the place alive
with laughter and misbehaviour, and then I scream.

Billy Collins

Knife and Fork

It is mid morning
and there are many pieces of paper
to be picked up
from the desk and put down again,
perhaps moved from one pile to another.

There are envelopes
to be slit open
with a wood-handled bread knife
and other envelopes
to be sealed with the flick of the tongue.

A little dew is still on the grass
but already I am thinking
of evening
and the meal we will have together –
your stories about the people at the office,

my stories about the dog, the grocer,
our glasses filled with wine,
darkness clinging to the windows,
your fork in the air,
my knee pressing against the table leg.

Billy Collins

Evening

There must be an afterlife
I thought, as I lay under the evening sky,
a mix of gray, white, a sweet blue,

its low light flickering
in the high greenery of trees,
and a breeze pushing from west to east.

There has to be another one,
I thought as my pupils dilated
over the notion of a bottomless abyss.

I would never complain
about a dreary eternity,
even a sulfurous, purgatorial one.

As long as it continued forever,
I would be happy to walk,
or fly or whatever,

through the low-grade atmosphere
with nothing to see
nothing to do.

I could always remember
my long days and nights on earth,
and especially the evenings,

the old girlfriend
Of evening
with a soft cloud over her face.

I would never stop mooning over her –
the first glass of wine,
the match to the paper in the stove –

even if I were spinning in a void
even if I had to spend forever
nailed upsidedown to a star.

Billy Collins

The Horn

Time is moving slowly this morning,
a miniature locomotive
that must begin again from a dead stop.

The only other motion
is a fan rotating on the floor
and a record turning on a turntable,

a vinyl record that is so dizzy
it has taken to expressing
its dizzyness through jazz.

I close my eyes
and a horn walks around the room
in a set of second-hand, golden clothes.

Ben Howard

Nameless
from 'Dark Pool'

They're waiting for a day or two, my friends
In Templeogue, to name their newborn daughter.
Will she be Lily? Deirdre? Margaretta?
They're saying nothing, letting us remain
Pleasantly in suspense, and letting her
Who presently is nameless have her day,
Unburdened by the garment she will wear
On every future day, the heavy ulster
Which may or may not suit her temperament,
Her way of speaking or her coloration,
But will, for life, be hers to don or carry.
So let me celebrate, this Sunday morning,
The blessed freedom of an unnamed child.
And let me recognize, as best I can,
That infant's counterpart, who may yet dwell
In every mortal frame that walks the planet
And every smattering of skin and bone
That lies beneath a name inscribed in granite.
To write a letter to that nameless one
Who in myself appears from time to time,
Unmarked by passion or adversity
And all the ills to which the flesh is prone –
To write a letter, asking her forgiveness
Or failing that, her tolerance and grace,
Could be the occupation of a lifetime,
A project suited to my later years,
A correspondence worthy of the effort.
For now, I lift my cup to that small soul,
So full of cries but empty of a name,
Who soon enough will have not one but three,
Each name a gate, a portico, a window.

Ben Howard

Jack and Jill
from 'Dark Pool'

Who shall be nameless, goes the politic
Expression, leaving us to conjure out
Of reference and tone the missing persons,
Who may be nameless to their dying days
But nonetheless appear as living shades
Acting and reacting on that stage
We set before our eyes. What matter, now,
If swarthy Jack was really Anthony
And winsome Jill was really Madeline?
I think of them this morning, Jack and Jill,
Who sat across from me, as nearly joined
As any could be on a public bus
Jouncing down a street in Sandymount.
Oblivious of me, as of those others
Who read their paperbacks or sat in silence,
Jack and Jill were visibly enthralled
By what they had created, hand in hand
And lip on lip, its presence palpable.
I tried myself to be oblivious
But found my gaze returning to their faces,
So rapt were they in worship of their god.
That was thirty years ago or more.
And though those devotees have long since gone
To places I would rather not imagine,
They stay in memory as in a vase,
Where dried stems may yet arrest attention
And dried blooms remain without a name.

Ben Howard

Ducked
from 'Dark Pool'

    When does a common thing become a name
To be pronounced, intoned, interpreted,
Until the presence of the thing itself
Dissolves within the noise the noun is making?
That question crossed my mind as I was walking
In Stephen's Green on a Sunday afternoon,
Remembering the time I heard the word
Collective, liking its liquid consonants,
Its quiet vowels and its gentle burst
Of energy, as though a cloud had spoken.
Little did I know that in a word
So pleasing to the ear and to the tongue
There lived a history of violence,
A chronicle of griefs and deprivations,
Of manacles and chains and executions,
All in the name of some *collective* good
Which justified the evils it propounded.
What faith remains when names replace the things
Entrusted to their care? That afternoon,
The ducks in Stephen's Green were diving. Dipping
Into the water and out, in quest of tidbits,
They fit, or so I thought, their names: they *ducked*
And *ducked* again, their comic act restoring
An old congruity of word and thing,
As though the first to name those feathered shapes
Had got it right: had said what he had seen.

Eugene O'Connell

The Colour of Dereliction

The story of Denny Andy and his dog
Coloured our view of Araglen House,
As surely as the tinted sweet covers
We pulled across our eyes as children
Painted the world any shade we wanted.

So we could never look at the gables
Of his house without imagining them
As the beak of a *gearrchoc*, fully open
For flies from a mother bird
Desperate to satisfy its craving.

Denny Andy himself would boast
Of the farm that went down his throat,
And how the dog he went to search for
In the pubs the morning after a session
Was a ruse to cadge a cure for his failing.

He was refused at Aggies and he vowed
Never to darken the door of a pub again,
A promise he had time enough to savour
When his wife shocked the locality
By leaving him for a job in the States,

The roof collapsed after he died,
But the legend lingered to stain
Our view of a house that would
Otherwise be bleached by the weather
Into the standard colour of dereliction.

Wendy Mooney

Miss Delicious

I am the woman they cut in two,
A freelance circus magician's assistant.
In my sequined costume
And spangled tights
I duck the knives
And squeeze up tight inside the box that smells of jasmine
– As out of fashion in my choice of perfume as in
My passion for pygmies:
Those tiny men with blows
Aimed so low that they cannot hurt me
And who, if they desert me, I can say
Were too small for me anyway
And didn't deserve a girl like Miss Delicious,
The freelance circus magician's assistant,
Who takes risks with her life each night and still
Looks a delight at the end of the show,
And is known to make a most nutritious cheese sandwich
At bedtime
Before she lies beneath the pink frilled canopy
Her mother sent from Chester and prays
That the high-hat magician might love her one day:
"Let me be the diamond in his mind-field," she says,
"And death to all dwarfs who ever deceive me. Amen."

John McKernan

Dear Saint Anorexia

Please fry this poem
About knobby potatoes &

May your hard working angel buddies
Degrease & deliver me from the aroma
Surrounding this ode to grits & greens &

While you're at it
Preserve each soy bean & grain of rice
From its designated haiku
Of plum & egret pea & wine

Indulge my quest for silence
That can tolerate now only
The hum of seed corn in a wicker basket &
Its explosion in pellet mist
Two inches – no more – below ground zero

Edward Power

Grandfather's Egg

He brought home an echo
of the shell that blew him off his feet
and came out in egg-shaped relief
on his forehead. There it was
half-buried in the furrows under his hat-rim
like something unexploded
fused to bloody calm

Out in the garden
he straightened his shoulders
inspected sweet williams
counted the rows talked to them
in secret language of the shell-shocked

He took a stick to coils of briar
that began next door. Shuffled
among the laying-boxes
his face honeycombed
by chicken-wire

I wondered about the egg on his forehead –
was it all white and yellow
like the ones we ate for breakfast? –
but didn't dare to ask

One day they put grandfather
and his egg in a box
and let us look at him
before they put the lid on
it was bigger than ever
on his smaller face
I wanted to reach out and touch it
but I was afraid
his eyes might spring open,
the shell burst.

Peggy O'Brien

The Oracle

In Delphi, County Mayo –
And why not? – the priestess
Spoke beside a roaring fire,
Dispensing wisdom as she ate

A bloody big feed
Of tea and scones – ethereal,
Sweet, golden clouds, so light
It was all I could do to stop

Gorging on them, gaining
Weight because I couldn't not
Celebrate someone in the kitchen
With the artist's touch.

Oh, I know it wasn't she
Who spoke, though every bite
Released a torrent. It was my love,
A man I haven't landed yet

And probably never will,
A fisherman who sees the river
From the fish's point-of-view
Inside out, and from the bottom up.

Indeed, his brown eyes weren't
His own. As he began to speak,
I saw bog water bubbling up
Oracular on elevated ground,

Then falling headlong down
A mountainside, sheer and bare,
Wild, white hair straggling
Demented over skin and bones.

It can take whole oceans
Of air to bring the crime to light,
Such distance from the hidden source
To make a river speak.

And this is what the Delphi
River told me, though I've never
Fished: the line is your nemesis
And only hope, your one link

With the dark life all around you:
Quick, slippery, swimming shapes,
Which you will die, never
Be satisfied, unless you hook.

Know also, mark, the secret
Of success is in the tension:
Too slack and you won't feel
A strike telegraphing down the pole;

Too tight and you may as well
Broadcast to the fish outright
Your intentions. (Lies often
Betray themselves with straightness.)

Cultivate a vague awareness.
Cast upstream and watch
Your fly drift willy-nilly,
More or less naturally downstream

Like a twig or an actual insect
On the water's surface; and, if
The line begins to belly out
Or coil, reel in the excess

Quickly. If the line gets caught
In a current in the middle of the river,
Suddenly goes taut, begins
To drag like rocks or a corpse,

Correct the situation on the spot:
Mend your ways, a few deft
Flicks will loosen matters up.
At least appear natural.

Just remember, as you stand there
Hour after hour, casting and
Recasting, waiting for the rending
Jerk of flesh on steel

Nobody knows why a salmon
Feeds so far from the open
Sea. It's a mystery why
A breeding fish rises to a fly.

Stand on the shore of Doolough,
Looking north over that black slab
Up through a Valley of Death,
Hear the awful, human howling.

The salmon is born to remember
An unappeased, unappeasable hunger.
Why else return? For a generous
Spoonful of glistening, cryptic eggs?

Mike Casey

A Splinter Of Light

Unlike migrating birds
We have no destination
And our journeys are broken
And disturbed.
Though resurrection
Is a hopeful tale
It turns on aspiration
And reason judges it of no avail.

The superlative gift
Will be reclaimed in time.
Knowledge, enlightenment, love
All you have learnt in a lifetime,
Will be irrecoverably lost.

An animal's eye holds no fear
But we alone know it is a stone's throw
From Eden to Gethsemene.
We watch our cell mates
Go down the passage one by one

And though we try to disbelieve
That someday it will be our turn to leave
We wonder when our hour will come
To put an end to what we are and could become.

We have no choice coming in
And none going out – save one.

Mike Casey

Geologists

The world is truly their oyster, especially in fossil form.
In jeans and open-toed sandals they travel to the ends of the earth
With their little silver hammers and poacher satchels of scuffed leather.

They chip away at sedimentary time, read waves of strata like music scores
And tap into the fossil archive for stories that will become epics.

They can be seen squatting on haunches in rust-coloured canyons
Or on the blue Himalayan plains, poring over lapidary tales
Whose endings are light years away and can never be explained.

The world has remade itself many times over, a new balance
Following every epidemic upheaval. We survived because
Of startling coincidences incredible without faith.

The ideographic rocks cannot speak the psalm of language
Or grace us with self-knowledge, yet we must be grateful
To these grizzled men who inspect the earth, prospecting
Not for gold but for the scripture of ancient stone.

Angela Bourke

Parallel Resources

Greagóir Ó Dúill, *Rogha Dánta 1965-2001*, Cois Life / Coiscéim, 2001, pb, €15
Biddy Jenkinson, *Rogha Dánta*, Cork University Press, 2000, cloth, €12.75

Two new volumes with almost identical titles, *Rogha Dánta*, "Selected Poems", testify to the healthy state of writing in Irish. Greagóir Ó Dúill's selection spans a youthful lifetime – 1965-2001 – drawing on his eight collections published by Coiscéim since 1981, and adding two poems previously unpublished. It is preceded by a thoughtful essay in which Ó Dúill traces his life in poetry and meditates on the influence on it of the preoccupations of his Doyle and Dempsey forebears and his parents' migration north of the Border when he was a child. Like the essay, the poems are restrained, but confident, contemporary and precise, cerebral but tender. 'Athrú Datha' begins with black-and-white Friesian cows seen from a train window and becomes a poem on Brown: *Donn*, the colour of cows long ago and of fresh-cut turf slipping from a young boy's grasp, it is also the name of the god of the underworld, the Lord of Time. Some of the poems, from *Saothrú an Ghoirt* (1994), are tiny Irish *haiku*, 'Leis Féin', a glimpse of a man sowing oats, recalls the Donegal of the poet's friend Cathal Ó Searcaigh:

> Fear ag cur síl i ngoirtín coirce,
> De chaitheamh láidir láimhe, boise, méara á scaipeadh.
> Leis féin a luigh ariamh.

In 'Coinnle Samhna', by contrast, a flowering field of light on a Dublin pavement ('gort de bhlátha solais') commemorates the environmentalist Ken Saro-Wiwa and eight other Ogoni executed in Nigeria in 1995 (not 1955), after opposing the activities of Shell Oil in the Niger Delta.

Rogha Dánta 1965-2001 is a collaboration between the long-established publishers Coiscéim and relative newcomers Cois Life. The clock-face on the cover by Eoin Stephens aptly illustrates the measured words within. With its coral-pink endpapers, legible, attractive typeface and judicious use of crimson print in the opening pages, it is a lovely volume; the occasional proof-reading errors may be corrected in the next edition.

Rogha Dánta from the poet known as Biddy Jenkinson contains no autobiography or *apologia*, nor does it represent her own choice of her work. The output of this elusive and sometimes enigmatic poet has instead been distilled into a happy sampler by Seán Ó Tuama and Siobhán Ní Fhoghludha, discerning critics and self-effacing editors.

Biddy Jenkinson has published four collections since 1986, when *Baisteadh Geintlí* ('Pagan Baptism' – or, perhaps, 'Circumcision'), announced the arrival of a shyly surreal imagination and a wicked intelligence, both highly original and gently subversive. Steeped in the literary traditions of the Irish language; alert to news, current affairs and science; widely travelled; amply lived, her work elasticises the rigid categories of metre and convention which have been so comprehensively studied but are so little practised. These poems are at once playful and disciplined; heady dances of meaning, generous with rhyme and rhythm, they double back on themselves and seem to belong to geological time, or to ancient manuscripts, as some of their own motifs suggest – even when mixed among images like the busy 2CV in the wryly scatological 'A.D. 1987'.

Several variations on the theme of lullaby make for surprising transformations. 'Mo Scéal Féin – Á Insint ag Aisling' moves from tender contemplation of husband or lover asleep to the chagrin of "Taise bhocht nimfeamáineach" – a woman sexually, eloquently, frustrated. 'Ciúnas', in three regular quatrains, is a love-poem from mother to infant in the style of Classical Irish poetry. 'Seoithín Seothó' is darkly lyrical, while 'Suantraí na Máthar Síní' blends Irish proper names, baby-talk and nursery-rhyme rhythms with the exotic historical atrocity of footbinding in China:

> Tá clabhcaí faoi Chlíona
> Tá spága faoi Mháire
> Tá Peigí spadchosach
> 's leifteáin faoi Niamh
> Deasaigh a stóirín
> mo lámh ar an bhfáiscín
> mé Maimín do leasa
> dod chumhdach le cion.

Dán na hUidhre (1991) whose title echoes that of the 11th-century vellum manuscript *Lebor na hUidre* (known in English as "The Book of the Dun Cow"), is Jenkinson's most daring collection, time-travelling from suburban Dublin to the voracious excesses of medieval saga. *Rogha Dánta* includes its title poem, a contemplation of the lines of scribal text and illumination which accommodate a hole in the vellum where a fly must have hatched from beneath the cow's skin. The poem escapes from the topology of its own text, giving back to the page its three-dimensionality as object and creating a new and dizzying picture.

Five more poems from this collection celebrate the unforgettable Mis, grieving carnivorous madwoman of medieval Irish saga, who has left the world of cooked food for a life in the raw in every sense. Countering all images of domesticity, Mis is the wild *alter ego* in Jenkinson's poetry as Sweeney is in Seamus Heaney's. 'XXX' opens with a woman observed asking for a marrowbone at the butcher's counter in Superquinn, Blackrock, Dublin, on a noisy, crowded Saturday, and progresses down the escalator as she chews on it. The shopping-centre's water feature becomes a *fualacht fian*, an outdoor cooking-pit in the forest where Mis's lover Dubhrois will cook for her and restore her sanity. The comically heroic scale of their embrace has echoes of Flann O'Brien's *At Swim-Two-Birds*, which itself echoed James Joyce's picture of the Citizen in *Ulysses*. The poem is something quite unique, however. It ends with graffiti on the shopping-centre wall: 'Mis XXX Dubhrois'.

Biddy Jenkinson and Greagóir Ó Dúill are very different poets, but common themes emerge. These retrospectives show none of the bitterness of alienation and loss found so often in the generation of Seán Ó Ríordáin and Máirtín Ó Direáin, and none of those poets' rejection of English-speaking Ireland. Both of these writers enter the new millennium embracing their east-coast antecedents while asserting an entitlement to write in Irish, and celebrating the privacies and expansive possibilities offered by the sometimes secret language whose resources they continue to explore. Well-read and well-travelled, they have developed parallel responses to globalisation and to the obscene state-sanctioned violence of our times. Ó Dúill's 'Coinnle Samhna' and Jenkinson's frozen lament on the Gulf War, 'Eanáir 1991', and its sequel '15 Eanáir 1991', find in the Irish language a path away from Newspeak.

Michael Massey

Kate At Two

Our faces,
inches apart,
are clouds
loaded with electricity
at the end of a humid day.

My face is cradled in your hands.

Grey bristles tickle palms:
small, warm; skin so soft
it's scarcely felt.

My grey eyes
that once were blue
before the years washed all colour out
look now into your dancing browns,
thrown wide open like a window;

and like a window
when the light is right
I see myself
looking back at me,

waiting for the smile
that sparks the explosive laugh
as love flashes between us,
earthing itself.

Eibhlín Nic Eochaidh

What she remembers now

is her ironic recognition
of the plant edging the path
in the garden – helxine, baby's tears;

the way two Irish accents made her head turn,
the narrow stairway to the upper room
and a familiar waiting, shuffling round the walls;

how she registered "after" by absence
of the travel poster on the ceiling:
last thing her eyes had seen "before".

Incommunicado
with apologies to Michael Hartnett

Disappointment, uninvited, steps
in between us; stretching
its metal, silver screen
where words and thoughts
like summer midges, or night-
time moths of black and red,
beat and batter their wings,
         exhaust themselves;
never making it through
from one side to
the other.

Eibhlín Nic Eochaidh

Before I left

she offered me a gift;
forcing me to choose
between three stones:
one flat and flaky,
a metallic shine – mica
maybe, or is it schist? –

second, hard to see – clear
vision gone – impression
of a regular shaped stone
stamp or tablet, edges smooth.

Third is coral coloured,
rose-soft, granite-hard:
this I choose.

Now I am living
to regret it;
rejecting binary oppositions
even when they co-exist
as in this stone:
light switches going off and on,
separate doors I used
to enter by and exit.
Now I want one door that swings
open in and out – a door
in a country & western saloon.

I want to learn
to time it right,
the going in
and coming out,

as when I stood in a young girl's body
rocking with the rhythm, anticipating
the returning arc
and slapping stroke of
skipping rope, hitting
bare cement.

Declan Collinge

Tine Gheimhridh
Do Mhairéad

Spréachann sméara an chuilinn
Lasmuigh ar dhuilleoga bioracha:
Istigh sa bhothán sléibhe
Ciúiníonn sioscarnach bloic tua
Faobhar na gríosaí mire
Is muirníonn fuisce te
Ár lámha spréite.

Ní paisean go tine dhearg
Ar scáthán ár súl:
Os ár gcionn
Téachtann rachtaí an tí
Faoi bhrat seaca
Agus bagraíonn muca sneachta
Ar 'chuile bhealach éalaithe.

Winter Fire
To Margaret
translation of 'Tine Gheimhridh'

Outside, the holly berries
Flame on jagged green;
Inside the mountain cabin
The whispered sibilance of logs
Calms the raging embers
And hot whiskey
Soothes our cupped hands.

Without blazing fire where
Is the passion reflected in our eyes?
Above our heads
The rafters stiffen in the frost
And snow drifts menacingly
Sealing every exit.

Matthew Fluharty

Late winter notes

Sore-throated February still life, fever-sick, untethered,
walking the bog road through Clonbarra.

The bell at the string's end of winter is lost,
confused with the strange demands of wind on rock,

water on oak, rough gale on the mute simplicity
of gorse.

And I don't care about words or images anymore.
Narrative is as hopeless and saturated

as the pastoral.

The season is all directions. This way: *cnoc fola*.
That way: the sea, a blue-green,

white-blue on the horizon.

cnoc fola: *the bloody foreland; the red hillsides along the coast outside of Gweedore in Co. Donegal*

Gerard Smyth

Hoard

In the museum that's a mystery to us
there is too much
of the hush of antiquity.
The loot of excavation, artefacts of yesteryear
divided into epochs,
tucked into the somnolent atmosphere.

The books of dogma,
the Crusader's sword
crafted to finish what Christ began.
Nothing can be touched,
the patriot's gun,
the carbon-dated skeleton and skull.

The keeper of the ossuary
moves among shadows that are simple to break.
Relics and chalices,
what was sunken but saved.
The metals of coinage,
hand-embroidered Huguenot lace.

Van Gogh

With all your strength you kindled
and quenched the starry night,
mixed the pigments it took to paint
the world you knew:
standing corn, potato-eater,
sower, reaper

and Gaugin's chair
pencil-sketched while you were
oblivious of all else.
Each self-portrait shows you
in repose and dying a little
or sometimes sick with longing
for a new life
away from sunflower and cypress.

Robert Greacen

Lord Kelly

The Times Obit buried him in superlatives –
Lord Kelly, icon of the Establishment,
Lauded by the great and good, an authority
On osteomyelitis, a bigwig of medicine,
Hero of a thousand surgeries, adroit fixer.
All that and more, yet for me he's simply Jim,
A whey-faced lad, scorned by his schoolmates,
Jostled in the playground, a cornered boy.
A new master once, writing down our names,
Asked Jim to spell his out. He mumbled:
'K-E-double L-Y, James K*a*lly.'
'Ah,' said the master, 'like the French town.'
Lickspittles, we sniggered in *schadenfreude*.
Years on, I heard that Jim was a doctor.
'You're joking – surely not Jim K*a*lly?'
Upwards he soared: pundit in Harley Street,
Consulted by dukes and princes, people said,
A fluent advocate for his profession,
Then an M.P. for a Royal borough.
He scooped up a knighthood and a peerage.
Only the Order of Merit eluded him.
Not bad, not bad at all for our Jim K*a*lly.

William Oxley

The Alchemy of Making

The day came down in a hurry
as if it was full of love
and I was talking to her again.

The awkward windy nights of unlove
above the bottled streets
were gone. Gone, too, the striving

lives of friends and their untender
ambitions. In place again
the vital unwrenched myths

of thought, made timeless
by her demanding smile
mixing moonlight and sunlight

in equal measure, inviting
the alchemy of making.

Colour To The Town

Fogherty wasn't one
      as you'd miss in the least,
for among men and women he was
      'lawless as a beast'.

But for all that, for all
      he was colour to the town,
and the snarl and sneer of him
      was lost when they sent him down.

Janice Fitzpatrick-Simmons

The Long Way Home

1.
You were lucky, you died at home,
after my long fight with hospitals
and administrations. You died
after much labour and in my arms.
Our son's long torso stretched
beside you, the music you made
of your life played on the tape-deck
in the room I made for you.

For me, everything about your care
pinned to the moment when your hand
loosened its hard grip on mine; the life
you loved so well closing down
to a final expression of exhaustion.
Here was the great man bowed –
death the leveller with his
locked jaw.

2.
It was Midsummer's Eve,
the grey mists had lifted its shroud
from the hills a little and a salmon light
caressed the grasses rippling in the wind.
The Angel of Death, his finality was in the room.
How many minutes passed before I flung the wide
doors open? Your breath bruised the room
and fled like a thrush underneath leaves
of sycamore and ash. Something
was going home.

The body must be prepared.

3.
What is a political act
against corrupt systems and dictators
and swaggering bigots all rife
in human endeavour; alive in Governments
and Hospitals, in Universities and Institutions?
Today a man died at home, his family wept beside him.

Janice Fitzpatrick-Simmons

Taking Names

The first wallpaper I ever chose was blue roses
because of Mary wrapped in the colour of sky
and crowned with stars. She looked like what
I knew of love, beautiful and sorrowful; beautiful
in the grotto at *the stations*, the water falling down,
the man made spring flowing up from faucetts
underground. Walking the cold stations in Framingham
Massachusetts is how I first came to Lourdes
and took the confirmation name of Bernadette.

The snow is deeper here in Ireland
this New Year's Eve of 2001. I work in
service to my husband, incontinent and wheelchair bound
because love and duty are so big in my heart that there is no choice.
And I wonder about the blackbirds, sparrows and meadow larks
who eat my bread, about their nests of feather and grief, about
that sacred peasant girl, about miracles and what it means to take a name.

Bones

After many days of rain
I've left home and your mists,
the mourning earth, the white
lilies of gravesides.

Over a harbour I shelter watching
the sun come from between clouds,
the rolling pewter and silver of a calm
sea swaying like a pendulum. Arctic Terns
and Black-backed Gulls wheel busy with garbage,
picking the bones of carrion, pushing forward,
busy with the messy energy of life.

And you would like it Jimmy, things moving
on, a life for Ben and me, everything you were
at the centre of things.

John Sewell

Carnality / Five Beech Leaves

1

Forget cars, forget the last house (a white cat cosying the wall)
forget hesitation, clothes or niceties of language, forget
how your face looks, be something different under the leaves.

2

Something's turned the holly berries on, I'm in the wood
and loving it, that ripening of green to red: the elder
swart with berries, fronting me, without a stitch of leaves.

3

Instead of finding, in the thick of the wood, in
a chemise of woodsmoke – a Diana; a satyr
penis exposed, came at me from the mirrored leaves.

4

First, the Book of Breathings, the Book for the Traversing
of Eternities, then the Ceremony of the Opening of the Mouth:
prone, on bracken-down, poring waist-deep over lustred leaves.

5

My tablespoon of blue milk on the mossy bole: sunlight
on the silver trunk did it – made me pause in the clearing
to make my mark, then slip away between the leaves.

Harry Clifton

To My Wife

Imogen, straight as a die in a crooked world.
Just to look at you, soul-sister,
Threading your way through the maze of *Cymbeline*,
The ageless lies, the plots and counter-plots,
The blank verse speeches honouring chastity
Is to know slander.
                    When the curtain rises
And you find yourself out there, already too late,
Exposure is total, everything unreal
Yet terrifying. The audience in the know
Is faceless, blank, too far beyond the footlights
And the close-up dazzle of events
You half-understand. The politics? Mere stagecraft.
Chastity? A word for your good name
In an age of cynics. Iachimo, Posthumous,
Cloten – deck them out in modern dress
And sell their stories off, to the yellow press.

Shamming dead in the cave of transformations
Hide yourself, then. '*....nor measure our good minds
By this rude place we live in....*' Two bare rooms
For the down-and-out, the social reprobate,
As wild a place as any in that Britain
Before Christ. A typewriter, bearing witness,
Stammering out its vision of the truth
In widowhood. Forces, gathering
From abroad, beneath an alien caesar –
Earthly redemptions.
                    Yes, it will come again,
The hour of luck and personal vindication.
You will be loved in public for a while –
The hangman, temporarily frustrated
In the background, and the audience clapping,
Dematerialising, in its own abyss,
A whiff of smoke in your nostrils, from the auguries
Of the soothsayer, anxious as always to please.

Harry Clifton

North Great Georges Street

Never having lived here, except in spirit
Or by proxy, through lovers and friends,
I'm tense for anyone's reappearance
As the doors cannon to, and the aftershocks sound
On the opposite houses. Blind at both ends,

Dark, with a sense of falling away
I could never probably stand my ground,
Not now, in that state of mind
Where a woman of twenty-six, between boyfriends,
Laying out possessions, never intending to stay,

Takes out a lease, some five floors up from the
   street,
And the night-machinery, the lights
Of Dublin Port and Docks, the whiff of coal,
The shuntings at the railhead, tons of freight,
Drive their wedge of iron into her soul.

An hour has struck, for moral loneliness
(May it never come back
after all this time...) A quartz clock
On the night-table, clothes in a gunny sack,
And sanctuary, for a while, from the middle classes –

One at work on a shooting-script, another painting
   tiles,
Another scraping cello-lessons, tiring after a
   while,
A woman with a baby on her own,
A man who broke down nightly, keeping a band on
   the road
I limit myself to those I have known,

Who found themselves far out on the learning curve
For once in their lives,
Alternative; who changed, or lost their nerve,
And now are household names, or public men,
Or vanished, and have never been heard of again,

Or may, for all I know, be living here
To this very day, through heightened windows
Eyeing me, for a rival or a peer,
A lover, who once slept over,
Returning to the unfinished business of years.

Harry Clifton

Hereafter

> *Perhaps only he who wants to, finds eternity.*
> —Eugenio Montale

They say, under certain conditions,
And maybe sleep is one of them,
The soul rises out of the body
And wanders about. And lying here
In the depths of the night, I hear him
Or his ghost, the old metronome
Of footfalls on the ceiling above me,
Unearthly stations, fiddled with,
Tuned into, or the sudden rush
Of cistern water, as an aged man
Relieves his prostate in the small hours.
They say his wife died long ago.
I was not here then. They say
There were children, or relatives,
So maybe it is one of them
Come back, days after the event,
To straighten things out. Or his own soul
Going about unfinished business
As ever, unopened correspondence
From his letterbox, collective memory,
The State, not letting him go just yet.
And the restaurant where he died,
The one at the corner, has to be paid.
Two days after, wreaths on the landing,
Rumours. That is all I know –
The rest visions, reported sightings,
Local history. Man overboard
In the great sea of eternity
Where, maybe, he just potters about
As always, within earshot,
Thinly partitioned from the living,
Neither in heaven, nor in hell,
Revisiting, under certain conditions –
Restless leg, or alcohol in the veins –
Those of us without souls to lose
With news of the huge anti-climax.

Tom Halpin

The Obstinate Quest

Thomas Kinsella, *Collected Poems*, Carcanet Press, pb stg£14.95, hb stg£29.95

Contemplating Thomas Kinsella's new *Collected Poems*, and the extraordinary career and achievement it represents to date, one is reminded of the percipience of some of the most positive critical judgements of his work up to the late '60s and early '70s – when he was at about "the middle of the journey", and immediately before his descent into the Peppercanister Poems, that still ongoing epic Work in Progress. Writing in the late '80's about her discovery of Kinsella's *Downstream and Other Poems* during the 1960's, Eavan Boland remembered that what had chiefly struck her in that volume was its "tone of...obstinate quest, the search of a dislocated intelligence determined to find some order and suspicious of what he finds as soon as he finds it. A tone, in other words, which...is resolutely modernist." This suggests what might be called the motivating force of Kinsella's poetic career and the unwavering spirit of agnostic integrity with which he has pursued it, his relentless exploration of continuously new forms and structures within which to accommodate his most pressing themes, especially since the '60s, each advance 'A New Beginning' in a "series of beginnings", of "developing and abandoned purposes." And in the early '70s, in an essay which surveyed Kinsella's development up to the publication of *Notes from the Land of the Dead* (1972), Robin Skelton claimed that the poetry possessed "a Dantesque grandeur and an intellectual authority" which made Kinsella "one of the very few living poets who can be said to be tackling the highest poetic task – that of creating a vision which makes sense of our universe." This suggests what might be described as the ultimate goal of Kinsella's poetry, then and since, whatever the modifications in practice such an ideal has been continually made to undergo by means of the more exploratory formal procedures implied by Boland.

Nevertheless, as far back as the early 1960's, he was admitting to a strong temperamental attraction to the kind of writer whose work sought to realise itself as a "conscious constructed fabrication of the human mind and intellect". Hence the importance throughout his poetry – but particularly the Peppercanisters – of his evocation of figures such as Plato,

Eriugena, Dante, Diderot, Mahler, Jung and the monumental achievements associated with them. In the variety of complex ways in which these figures inhabit the poetry, they do so as exemplary or admonitory presences in relation to Kinsella's own massive undertaking, as if he is measuring, testing his aspirations against their secure achievements. But if this feature of his work indicates its profound seriousness of purpose – "creating a vision which makes sense of our universe" – and brings to mind Yeats's image for his work as "a monument of unageing intellect", it also, as often as not, strikes an ironic self-mocking note with regard to what the whole enterprise amounts to ("suspicious of what he finds as soon as he finds it"). Think of the way in which *Ulysses*, while offering itself, albeit obliquely, as the "epic of today's Ireland", also sends itself up as "this chaffering, allincluding most farraginous chronicle." Likewise, "the whole thing" – a recurring phrase of Kinsella's suggesting both the raw material of experience and the work wrought from that material – is mocked by a poem which plays with that phrase in its title, 'The Entire Fabric' (*One*, 1974), where the undertaking is exposed as amounting to no more than a contrived affair of smoke and mirrors. Watching from afar are "The Shades…in their noble chairs" – Kinsella's exemplary guides – taking stock of the shambles being perpetrated below them. "I lift my / baton", he writes in *Her Vertical Smile* (1985), as he mounts the podium in emulation of Mahler, "and my /trousers fall."

Even so, Kinsella's work has continued to grow inexorably in scope and scale, as if thriving on the tensions generated between those two poles of Yeatsian high seriousness and Joycean self-irony. And among the reasons for its continued growth must surely be the major formal reorientation it began to undergo from the early '70s as the result of his deepening appreciation of Ezra Pound's *Cantos* (for "their extraordinary scope, their reliability in local detail, their capacity to keep going," and William Carlos Williams' *Paterson* (for its "creative relaxation in the face of complex reality"). Their examples in particular made him realise "that the modern poet has inherited wonderfully enabling free forms…which ought to be felt as a whole rather than in…stanzaic expectations", and this confirmed him in the new direction his work had already begun to take since the early '60s with longer poems and sequences (*Moralities*, 'Downstream', *Wormwood*, *Nightwalker*, 'Phoenix Park') gradually displacing the shorter, lyric form – the "well-wrought urn" – which had predominated during the first decade or so of his career. With the appearance of the first Peppercanister in the early '70s he had effectively committed himself to a conception of poetry which he would later describe a "totality that is happening, with the individual poem a contribution to something accumulating."

This volume continues that resistance to closure which the open, fluidly interlocking forms of the Peppercanisters have made such a crucial feature of his poetry for over thirty years now. The five Peppercanister booklets which have appeared since the publication of *Collected Poems 1956-1994* are included, illustrating not simply another phase in the unfolding Work in Progress (inaugurated by *The Pen Shop* (1997) – nightwalker in daylight!) but also Kinsella's apparently inexhaustible fertility of formal experiment, poetic organisation and linguistic texture. Yet for all the astonishing variety of these, and other features of the writing which this volume displays, it also reveals an impressive thematic unity: his preoccupation with love, death and the artistic act has been consistent since the beginning of his career. Indeed, it was in large part to foreground the increasing importance of those themes as his work evolved from its earlier, largely lyrical 'closed' forms to its later, sequential 'open' forms that he subjected so much of his earlier work to radical culling and revision in his 1994 *Collected Poems*. The opportunity provided for a sustained review of his entire corpus by the preparation of such a collection enabled him to bring his beginnings as a poet into a more precisely calibrated alignment with the constantly changing dynamics and shape of the work as an emerging whole, and the complex system of internal, subtly interlocking and increasingly refined relations it had come to be governed by ("a system of living images/making increased response / to each increased demand"). This latest collection exhibits even further refinements, with the elimination of yet another poem from the '50s and two from the early '70s.

Some years ago, Kinsella expressed the hope that his work would, in the end, represent "a meaningful model for the life lived" (showing the "Growth of a Poet's mind", if you will). This is to be reminded of how intensely and unremittingly autobiographical the sources of his poetry have always been, paying the closest possible attention to the successive stages of human growth and development as represented by the experiences of one individual (albeit of immense gifts and intelligence) from childhood through adolescence to maturity, marriage, parenthood and grandparent-hood. Not the least striking feature of this handsomely produced volume (nearly 380 pages in length) is the design on its front cover of a streetmap of part of Dublin's inner city around James's Street and Guinness's Brewery, Swift's Hospital and the Grand Canal Harbour, an area close to where Kinsella himself was born and where his parents and grandparents had lived. His imaginative excavations over the years of this place and its inhabitants, in biographical and autobiographical, in historical and psychic terms, have created some of the deepest and most electrifying resonances in his always resonant output. It is also where, as a schoolchild, that his evolution as the poet he has become began, when "The taste / of ink off / the nib shrank your / mouth." ('Model School, Inchicore', *Songs of the Psyche,* 1985).

Mary O'Donnell

Necessities

Time for pruning, my annual appointment
in the garden. Poised to cut back and trim,
I interrogate trees on the question of excess,
argue in favour of vigour, the prospect
of uncluttered grace. Light is honey-coloured,
flows in rivulets over lingering shoots,
bathing piebald autumn, skewed leaf, the flaccid rose,
preparing them to yield. The garden's specked foils,
dazzle of spice red stems, saffron garments,
await the merciless crange, my diligent cut
an act of kindness for the sake of sleeping shadows.
It grips neatly, encloses the resistant wood until
my shoulders strain, then the swift short passage
as metal meets metal and the bough snaps and tumbles.
One morning, long after old branches have burned,
I will look out, watch how trees calibrate growth,
the bonds of excess, the need for death.

Holy

Every venerable ancient seeks out his body,
every ancestor who once struggled
and, themselves inhabited, dwells there.
He almost weeps each time we leave,
then laughs through fear of this encounter
that nothing, no-one, can lift.
His frailty, a habitation for the wise and good,
is suffered in by a suffering god
who waited for a time, a moment,
patient while this son lived in the vastness
of life's green garment, exploring its folds.
Now he draws it down, tightly, closer,
so that the spirit, that vast, tumbling
greenness, the momentous motion of every cell
of his eighty years, are no longer divided,
but live intimately and as one.

Mary O'Donnell

Field Work

The rats and crows are feasting.
Big winds rotate above the half-cut corn
and every hour is a breath
drawing closer to completion.
In the garden, phloem seeps from stems
and pickings, two kittens cavort
around jungles of mint and mottled daisies.

We know the season has shifted,
that autumn's in-drawn breath
has entered crevices where sun once lingered,
a summons to gorge on sweet apples,
to trim dipping boughs, burn curling leaves.

While rats and crows exult beneath the wind,
stuffed with golden seed,
we heed the breath of suffering, hearing huge clappers,
the approaching, relentless thresher,
blades spinning at sunset,
the rustle of tumbling husks,
kernels borne away by the encroaching dark.

Máiríde Woods

The Magic Tablecloth

She pressed it on me as I leapt into his car,
A godmother's gift. A bit of an embarrassment.
It'll see you through
Hard times, she told me. Just shake it out
Once, twice and thrice. The trick is
Not to use it too often.

The first time I unfurled it my purse was empty
But there was sweet cake and honey and you
Among the crusty loaves. A singing fairy feast
Never repeated. The next time
The lemonade was flat. Even magic
Has its off days.

Today there are gaps everywhere.
Holes in my finest voile, mould on the rosewood.
Children and lovers
Have vanished like strawberries
And even the spell of memory
Is powerless to restore them.

Still, I keep my tablecloth carefully
Tissue paper and all that jazz. In times of sorrow
I stroke its damask folds, but keep myself
From shaking them out.
Perhaps next year. In Jerusalem. Or somewhere.
Before I die.

Fred Johnston

Syllables on a White Wall

Kevin Kiely, ***Plainchant for a Sundering***, Lapwing Publications, pb, €3
Eiléan Ní Chuilleanáin, ***The Girl Who Married The Reindeer***, Gallery Press, hb €17.50, pb €10.
Tom French, ***Touching The Bones***, Gallery Press, hb €17.50, pb €10.

Kevin Kiely did good work in introducing new writers by his editorship of the new writing pages in *Books Ireland*. His own writing has always been exotic, daringly fragmentary; as if life, being similarly fragmented, could not be caught or described in a pattern. It's difficult not to view all of the poems here as being sections in one long poem whose template is the break-down of relationships and self. The individual poems are blistering with the heat of the events stoked up within them: these are urgent, gut-worked stanzas, misshapen, argumentative, declarative.

Kiely's style – and the liberty of his voice – has more to do with those few Irish poets who have been exposed to a working European modernity; the work is given its head, allowed to find its own form. This is dark, almost Gothic stuff, not for the poetically squeamish:

> we'll have to get you on one or other scheme,
> suggests Doctor C,
> first we must try and find out what's been going on
> we no longer deal in mental illness
> Jeffrey Masson the U.S. anti-psychiatrist
> Looks for suitable models of interpretation . . .
>
> ...a breaking, a sundering, a separation not
> unlike between two people...
> –'The Head Doctor'

There is more than a touch of the openly confessional about the work here, and in some poets that has become a sort of literary affliction, disabling them from sounding anything but weary and wearying. I am mindful of Micheal Smith's remark in a recent *Poetry Ireland News* that "Poetry as therapy is another matter. And that should be considered in the area of clinical psychology, not aesthetics." True. There are dangers in tossing one's own cumbersome emotional baggage at the feet of a reader. A certain transcending magic must be worked to make it acceptable beyond itself. Poetry is not, after all, a horror-story. Nor is it an analyst's couch, with the reader as analyst.

I think the internal energies of these poems permit Kiely to get away with it, for one slim collection at least; the voice here sings a warning of the disunity of ourselves as individuals when seemingly 'joined' to another person, how the individual remains his or her self, free to make decisions or be obliterated by them without the other's consent: "In bed sometimes we found a union beyond our daily/strife but could not blend the two..." ('Nora's Wedding') A grim reality, and consciousness of reality, stalks these poems. In an acutely aware state, as all lovers are at points of desperation, even the heavens seem to intervene:

> I agree with your every condemnation of me
>
> then came the comet in that year –
> on Good Friday of ninety seven I left home
> with half-discussed plans of long leave...
> –'Nora's Wedding'

If Kiely offers any consolation in the face of the notion that love may be a delusion, a not-new idea that love is a form of sickness, then perhaps it is to point the sufferer in the direction of the poetic imagination and whatever transcending and healing it can do: the last word of the last line of the final poem in this collection is a name, "*Mallarmé.*" It may just as well have been Baudelaire. Congratulations to Belfast's enterprising little publisher, Lapwing, for taking on this collection.

Eiléan Ní Chuilleanáin is a poet of meticulous style and craftsmanship. The jacket-blurb, and for once it doesn't over-reach itself, describes her as 'a poet of perfect pitch', reminding us, as we occasionally need reminding, that poetry begins in music. One might go a tad further and say that her work gives lyric voice to the small, sad and ordinary in life without song;

> Did she know what she was at
> When she slipped past the garden door
> To palm the rolled notes from the teapot...
> –'Troubler'

Again, the ordinary, as Blake knew, is a door to transcendent perception.

> Where did I see her, through
> Which break in the cloud, the woman
> In profile, a great eye like a scared horse?
> —'From an Apparition'

A very fine poem commemorates the late and great Agnes Bernelle, whom I cannot say I knew but whom I met on several occasions, and who died in 1999. Bernelle's spider-like creativity is mapped neatly in the poem, where the spider itself is a living glyph of shadow:

> Her presence is the syllable on the white wall,
> The hooked shadow. Her children are everywhere,
> Her strands as long as the railway-line in the desert...
> —'Agnes Bernelle, 1923-1999'

In a two-poem section entitled 'Coda', reaffirming the musical, Ní Chuilleanáin reworks a poem from Langland's 'Piers Plowman' and a translation from the Irish of 'Kilcash', a late 18th century lament-poem, authorship unknown or uncertain; perhaps I'm confusing it with Raftery's 'Cill Aodáin'. But I'm almost certain I've heard an author mentioned somewhere.

Ní Chuilleanáin is a scholarly poet without a trace of pomposity or showiness, an unsettling rather than outrightly disturbing poet. There is a moving quietness, a reserve of sorts, throughout these poems which belies their often troubling directness. The ordinary is transfigured, magically and without fuss. It is the magic, the spell cast by these poems, which inserts itself in the complacent soul.

As befits a first collection, Tom French's *Touching the Bones* lifts up its petticoats and runs riotously all over the place. Thank God for it; I actually knew a critic once who attacked a poet for writing about 'everything'. French doesn't rein in this natural required first energy; the scrupulousness can come some other time. French seems to have been around longer than the publication of a first volume suggests; the list of acknowledged publications at the back seems to indicate that he's served a dutiful apprenticeship. Thankfully, French's voice can often rise in pitch: 'Pity the Bastards' is a sharp and almost elegiac commentary on the hopelessness and darkness of the human condition and reminds me, in style at any rate, of the poems of Roger Phillimore, a local poet in the Kinvara area who, to my mind, should be read:

> *Pity the bastards* who clamped buck rabbits' heads
> between their legs and funnelled *poitín* into them
> until they bucked, the wide sky shrivelling in their
> pissed eyes, who swore blind that spirits sweetened
> the meat...

In the end, and a touch predictably, we discover that French is compassionate and it comes as rather a disappointment.

As with so many poets whose first poetic yearnings were reared, so to speak, in the nest of a university, there is much here which may prove incomprehensible to the ordinary reader; references, ideas. It's hard to see the real world through too much academic clutter and there is every sign ('Pity the Bastards' is as good an example as any) that French may, indeed can, toss aside the poisoned cloak of arcane erudition and hit the real world at a run. 'Singing in the Underground' is dedicated to the memory of Jack Mitchell, a canny unrepentantly political Scot who was a fine folksinger; and 'The Botanic Gardens' is dedicated to Anne – 'Annie'– Kennedy, a modest, unassuming American woman I knew well for many years, a friend from the Rahoon days who had no time for cant or artsy 'image' and who wrote some decent poems, while being also a fine photographer – time, perhaps, for a revisiting of her work? Of Jack Mitchell, French says: "All nature seems to contradict the loss...", and for Anne Kennedy he lists names of flowers, as if showering them upon her memory. Poignant and real.

In general, French's work is exuberant and vital as it should be and intensely readable; he knows where the real is, even if, for most of us, it will not be found in "...that yarn about Pierre Bonnard / making his friend Vuillard distract the museum guard / while he produced his tubes of oils and palette knife / to touch his work up where it needed touching up." (' Bonnard's 'Coffee' '). He has a sure-footedness around his craft and the maturity of a much older practitioner. 'Hip' is a quite beautiful and simple lyric which becomes memorable: "I know when I hold that tidy heap / your hip displaces in the hollow / of my hand, I want, when all of this / is finished, my clay hand to be // resting on your clay hip..." French's ability to move from the fragile lyric sense to the outraged or socially sensitive is a very healthy sign in a poet. He will do good.

Tom MacIntyre

Le Premier Fauve

Different from birth – but did he
have to be *that* different, the feet
back-to-front, the hip not right,
rolling gait, gift of the gaffe.
Dad (if he was Dad) stares, Mom –
who's had hopes – develops an
exponentially expanding migraine.
One morning, they throw him out.

He's on fire, as would you, given
such disorder and no tomorrow.
He finds a forge, this was written,
an underground forge, also written,
bitten by, seems, a need to be
out of sight but within hearing.
Over dinner parental brows furrow –
'What's he at, our misbegotten Hotten-

tot?' Some din. Demented *Anvil Chorus*
from Verdi aeons before it's
due. He's possessed. Keeps company
with 'regressive types' – more than kin.
Women? They come and go, talking –
patient voices – of a 'glum interiority'.
Never had much success with women
but always women around – in numbers.
Meanwhile, what in thunder's going on
down there in the mother-mine?

Fasten seat-belts, please, the plane
bucks. He's making exquisite things,
born for it, the break-through, what
shakes everyone is the *naturalness*,
the more-life-than-life throb of his art.
Wreath, necklace, vase, Pandora –
whatever he touches glows. Period.
There has to be a catch. Yes. Feud

with Mom remains unresolved. Time,
he decides, now to settle her
hash, grits, and hominy *in nomine*
you name it. Designs a throne –
lovely touch there – that will bind
her fast, then – one with her moan –
levitate. The trap is sprung, Mom
hangs suspended in mid-air
on the ruffian son's trick-chair.
Now let her sizzle – the wagon.

Fog over 'Frisco, clamour in Heorot.
They send a heavy. The heavy's driven
back with heinous losses. Addle, Zeus
suggested, our dear maverick, note,
has never been on the batter, head down
for years, fixated, a man, a mission.
Throw me, said Dionysus, that thyrsus.

Hephaestus toiled. Sparks, soot, clang,
but still he heard a soundless step,
knew. Stands before him Mr October,
all curls, smiles, the loosest morals.
A sip? A glass? Try some more?
We've a widow's cruse – don't be shy.
Dionysus brings him home, senseless,
slung across the yearnful back
of an ass blind of one eye.

Did that same ass deloother
M. Heph. Vulcan Gobán, Esquire?
Morning, no one may him gainsay:
he'll free Mom – *La Divina*'s
all he wants, and no more bother.
O, you flighty flighty boy –
Hera (bless her) suppressed a sigh.
She strolls from her prison chair.
The room. The bed. Aphrodite.

It couldn't work. It doesn't – ever.
Maybe it's not meant to. He's
preoccupied – hammer, tongs, fire,
work, work, making the magic, well,
somebody has to, I suppose,
she takes up with his younger
brother, Ares, gets what she wants –
which wasn't, end of many a story,
just wasn't, the blacksmith's to supply.

Now what? He gets it bad – this
sound familiar? – for a strong woman.
Some – the usual – felt they were
well matched, she a woman
and a bit of a man, he a man
and so on. It's not to be –

stay your tears, better's to be,
the miracle, the marvel news,
we, with pleasure, air once more:
Athene side-steps him in a hot hour,
his sauce hits the earth, sends
shock-waves, impregnates, and the child,
the *wunderkind* of that happenstance

ordained union, founds the line
that shapes the city, Parthenon dreams,
invents the cello, chess, *cuisine
minceur*, takes us to the theatre
tonight – to show that we're alive,
to be talking to our friends.

Brian Donnelly

Making It New

Rita Ann Higgins, *An Awful Racket*, Bloodaxe Books 2001, pb£7.95
Mary Dorcey, *Like Joy In Season, Like Sorrow*, Salmon Poetry, pb £6.99
Catríona O'Reilly, *The Nowhere Birds*, Bloodaxe Books 2001, pb £6.95

These three collections reflect the variety of contemporary Irish poetry. They range from verses that communicate immediately and often memorably on a number of contemporary issues and personal traumas to the work of a young poet whose first collection reflects a sensibility and aesthetic that is inward, speculative, allusive. The poems embody aesthetics that range from the direct comment and naked confessional exploration to lyrics that rejoice in their own making.

Those familiar with Rita Ann Higgins's previous works will recognise that same mixture of unsentimental social observation, humour and controlled anger as she views the unpoetic landscape and lives on unglamorous housing estates. The most powerful poem in the book is 'Black Dog in my Doc Days', an elegy for a young man who committed suicide in which the blend of conversational intimacy and ritual structure is deeply affecting:

> When depression slept
> you were up for anything,
> go for it and you went for it –
> times you got it, other times you lost it,
> you didn't play the lyre,
> you played the horses,
> lady luck was often with you
> you never looked back
> William and Lara miss you.

Her strength is an ability to blend colloquial vigour within formal structures that shape and control emotions. In lyrics like 'Bare Bones', 'They Always Get Curried Chips' and 'An Awful Racket', ordinary lives are given their own voices. Occasionally, as in 'The Clemson Experience', the voice becomes forced and false. Here the satire on the institutional Ireland of literary conferences and golf clubs lacks subtlety. On the other hand when, as in 'They Never Wear Coats', the scene is the familiar one of women together, the observations are acute and the voice (this time a Newcastle one) exact:

> These tubes on legs,
> high heels on stilts,
> will paint the town red.
> A swig for you,
> a swig for me –
> 'that looks lovely on ya hinny,
> I'd nearly do ya meself.'

The two last poems in the collection show best the strength and range of Rita Ann Higgins's imagination. Each is an extended monologue that demonstrates this poet's capacity to invent other lives in idioms that are eccentric and distinctive. In 'They Never Clapped' she captures the frustration, humour and pathos of mothers who try to live vicariously through their young daughters; in 'The Jugglers', the voice is that of a single mother at her wits' end:

> 4: *The Clinic*
>
> I went up for help
> with the shoes and uniforms,
> that sort of thing.
> The woman at the hatch was a right fuckin wagon,
> she said I was in the wrong place.
> It took me two buses to get there.
> I asked her where was the right place.
> Try the Vincent de Paul, she said.
> When I got outside
> I cried with rage.

The language and tone of Mary Dorcey's *Like Joy In Season, Like Sorrow* is more formal and restrained though no less compelling, as the speaker comes to terms with her mother's ageing and physical decline. These lyrics range from the quiet drama of 'Making Small Talk' with its jagged, cryptic lines, to the beautiful, reposeful image of 'Landscape':

> Her eyes stare
> Into the distance.
> Her hands restless
> In her lap.
> Memories sprout
> From the fissures
> In her face,

> Like grass
> In a graveyard.

In 'Fairy Tales', she tenderly dramatises the reversal of the parent-child roles in a series of graphic images:

> Now, I lift your swollen feet
> From the basin and wrap them
>
> With a towel, in silence.
> Always dry between the
> Toes, you used to say. But
> I cannot. They are moulded
>
> Together, inseparable...

At their best such lyrics form a "window to the heart" – as in 'Frost', the most accomplished poem in the book, worthy of becoming an anthology piece:

> Damp has risen
> through the bare boards
> and seeped into
> your voice.
>
> And look –
> along the pathway
> that led to the sea –
> on the grass
> and on the hedges,
> a first frost has formed.
> It glitters on
> Your hair
> and skin.

Mary Dorcey's collection bears the imprint of middle-age, that time of life when the certainties of existence begin to disintegrate and death becomes an ever real presence. Caitríona O'Reilly's first book, by contrast, has the verve and excitement of life and language newly encountered. *The Nowhere Bird* is thematically eclectic and the variety of the poems reveals a natural talent experimenting and making a mark. The flowers in 'Daffodils' have a strange, preternatural presence that Wordsworth would scarcely recognise:

> They bring this hint of something startled in them –
> the dreadful earliness of their petals

> against dead earth, the extremity of their faces
> suggesting a violent start –
> dumb skulls opening, overnight, to vehemence.

At their best her poems have the clarity and quirkiness that achieves the ideal of the author of the *Lyrical Ballads*, whose verses aimed to clear the lenses of perception and to make us see the everyday with a new clarity of vision. Such is the case in poems like 'The Harbour in January' and 'Hide', where the landscape

> Seen from above
> the trees are guanoed sea-stacks in a greeny cove
> full of gulls' primeval shrieks and waves' extinctions.
> Here birds safely crawl between the bushes,
> wearing their wings like macs with fretted hems.
> The air's a room they fill to bursting with their songs.
> All day the common warblers wing it up
> and down the scale, see-saw, hammer-and-tongs.
> This is not aimlessness. It is something industrial.

The poems in this collection range from childhood memories and foreign landscapes to playful meditations upon natural phenomena. The technical variety of the verse is almost always assured, as in the seemingly effortless control of the speaking voice along the iambic line in 'Autobiography' and 'Thunder over the Humber', and in the finely shaped 'Augury', where the sonnet form frames a series of beautiful images of natural movements. 'Diary of a Conformist' shows best a poet possessed of a fine narrative gift founded on an assured interplay between the colloquial voice and formal control of the six line stanza:

> Later, when she switches off the light
> the willow-patterned wallpaper grows ears
> and eyes and tusks and trunks, while near
> the door are dogs with eyes like dinner-plates.
> Outside, Stephen's open-mouthed granny sits
> digesting wicked children as they pass her.

Not all of the poems in this book are this assured. But even in those lyrics where the conceits lose their bearings, the reader is aware of a writer with a rare gift for the memorable image and a seemingly effortless ability to explore and exploit the formalities of poetic structures.

Peter Kane Dufault

Scenario
"This war can go on for generations" – The White House

If, some millennia hence,
galactic *voyageurs*
blest with intelligence
should seek particulars

about a great oblate
spheroid of good locus
but long-since desolate
and toxic to the touch,

imagine the memo:
'seems there were *Humans* here –
Billions of them! ergo
they filled the biosphere,

crushing all creatures else,
and then turned on each other
with variant gospels
of brother murdering brother,

of nation murdering nation,
whole continents likewise...
A puzzling destination
to reach from Paradise.'

Denis Collins

The Parcel
(Runner-up in the Senior Category, SeaCat National Poetry Competition 2001 in association with Poetry Ireland)

It always arrived late,
two or three days after
St. Stephen's Day,
a great squashed box
with enough chalky brown paper
to cover all our school books
and string enough to tie
up every rose bush in Wexford.
As you opened it
the smell of America leaked out
and then bright coloured dresses
and light brown summer shorts
and a compendium of
eighty-two board games.

There was always a new coat
that made you look
like a gangster's moll
or a million dollars.
Somewhere in the bottom
there'd be a bunch of
Superman comics that had gotten
creased on their way over.

Between Christmas and
Nollaig na mBan
we had Xmas in Wexford,
a kind of hand-me-down America
wrapped in cardboard and string.

Merrily Harpur

The Lesson

(Runner-up in the Senior Category, SeaCat National Poetry Competition 2001 in association with Poetry Ireland)

Take off your coats — reverse yourselves
Like sleeves. I mean a second life,
Sharp as grief. An edge like liquefaction
Where back becomes bezel.

His chisels ordered in seraphic rank;
The Western saw that cuts on the push,
The Eastern saw that severs on the draw;
A reliquary for the steel square.

Sharpen was the word he never used.
For three days you tune tools
Learn ways to lap backs dead flat on
Two-forty wet-and-dry

Or the red diamond stone. On twelve-hundred
Hone bezels to the shine of fish,
Wipe off the burr, burnish them on
The Japanese water stone;

Talcum the strop and wound it twice.
Don't stop before you can shave your arm.
A life rich in metaphor, the vocabulary
That raised the cathedrals.

To be lords amongst these shaven ringlets, first
Be monks making tasks acts, he could have said,
Unmask grain, return its life to wood.
Instead he will demonstrate –

Doffing his glasses – the job and the kingdom.
As by a suitor the blade was offered:
As by a lover, minutely delayed: then
The wood drank the chisel.

Caroline Lynch

My Grandfather

(Runner-up in the Senior Category, SeaCat National Poetry Competition 2001 in association with Poetry Ireland)

My grandfather is lying like a newborn
And will be going into the earth soon.
His hands have lost their lifelines
Smoother than a baby's and papery
With no print on them
No soil on them.
Wrist deep in the fields
He took home his land beneath his fingernails
And each season turned in his palm
Winter turned in his palm.
Outside the ground is warming and rising
But the world in his hands has sunk away
The sun is going down and he is turning home
Away from the house and down to the fields.

Leanne O'Sullivan

Crescendo

*(Winner of the Secondary Schools Category, SeaCat National
Poetry Competition 2001 in association with Poetry Ireland)*

Driving to my Doctor in July, I sit
with my feet on the dashboard, calves
glinting in the white heat, a new lexicon crawling
around the corners of a napkin as I try to write
against my thighs. Above our red Toyota
the branches and leaves of Ireland have kindled
with the sky, a Monet where there was
once a Cézanne. My mother seeks out
the straightest routes, allows the car
to ebb the smooth middle of the road as
the wind laps the rim of the window, like
a staccato to the music of Cat Stevens.
I think she loves the passion of over-taking,
the thunder of engines flirting on opposite sides
of the road. The corners of her eyes
will sharpen. Her stomach will tense and flatten.
Lips taut, she takes the reigns of our
lives with both hands, and as I
close my eyes she delivers me
to the darkness just before birth, the pulse
of gears aroused, swelling, like the hum
induced by speed. We slide along
the vein of mom's road, our bodies moving
through the air like seeds through a pistil,
and when I can feel my hair whipping my jaw again
I open my eyes and glance at my mother,
strands of her hair tucking in the salty tattoo of the wind,
her elbow angling over the lip of the door.
We descend, sending loose chips
flying like progress. She drives faster and faster
as if she is driving to save my life.
We are falling through the green of Ireland
and mom has the gear-stick in her fist
as if it is the strong branch of a tree to cling to.
    I change stations on the radio,
touching her fingers.

Noel Monahan

The Funeral Game

*(Winner of the Senior Category, **SeaCat National Poetry Competition 2001 in association with Poetry Ireland**)*

That winter we came to terms with death.
Every shoe-box was a coffin
For anything small and dead
And we wrapped them in calicoes, velvets...

We grabbed hats, coats, umbrellas,
From the hallway to dress as mourners,
Someone struck an iron girder in the hay-shed
To sound the funeral bell,
John Joe beat the dead march on a saucepan.

We held wakes, issued death certificates
To old crows, kittens, chickens...
Lined the graves with stones,
Erected crosses with ash sticks.

We pretended to cry, struggled with our Latin prayers,
Filled the wet graves in the clover field,
Genuflected in the direction of a whin bush,
The rain pelting down,
We left by a side-gap,
Back to the hay-shed for tea , bread, butter...
For all who travelled long journeys.

Notes on Contributors

Ivy Bannister writes fiction, non-fiction, plays and poetry. She has received the Francis MacManus, Hennessy and Mobil Ireland Playwriting awards.
Angela Bourke teaches in the Department of Modern Irish at University College Dublin.
David Butler poems have appeared in a wide variety of journals. His poem 'Swallows' won the Ted McNulty prize in 2001.
Mike Casey's poems have been published in *Poetry Ireland Review*, *The London Magazine*, *Staple*, *The Bridport Anthology*, *The Sunday Tribune*, and elsewhere. He is the author of a novel, *Come Home Robbie* (O'Brien Press, 1990).
Harry Clifton has published five collections of poetry, all from Gallery Books, the latest being *Night Train through the Brenner* (1994). His short stories are collected as *Berkeley's Telephone* (The Lilliput Press, 2000).
Michael Coady's *All Souls* was reprinted last year, in a revised version, by Gallery Books.
Declan Collinge's collections are *Sealgaireacht* (Clóchomhar Teo, 1982), *Faoi Léigear* (Coiscéim, 1986), *Fearful Symmetry* (Mentor Books, 1990), and *Common Ground* (Inisfail Press, 1996). A bi-lingual poet, he is the author of the popular *Saibhreas* series of Irish textbooks.
Billy Collins is the author of six collections of poetry, including *Taking Off Emily Dickinson's Clothes* (Picador, 2001). He is currently serving as United States Poet Laureate.
Denis Collins poems are published in *The Waterford Review*, *Riposte* and *Poetry Ireland Review*, and elsewhere. He won the inaugural Francis Ledwidge Poetry Award in 1999, and featured in the 'Poetry Ireland Introductions' readings in 2000. He is the Director of THE WORKS publishing.
Tony Curtis has published four collections of poetry, the most recent being *Three Songs of Home* (Dedalus, 1998). A new collection, *What Darkness Covers*, is forthcoming. He is a member of Aosdána.
Gerald Dawe has published five collections of poetry, most recently *The Morning Train* (Gallery Books, 1999). He is currently completing a new collection, as well as working on *Mother Tongue: Collected Essays on Poetry and Politics in Ireland*.
Ted Deppe teaches at The Poets' House, Falcarragh. His most recent book is *The Wanderer King* (Alice James Books, 1996); *Cape Clear: New and Selected Poems* is forthcoming from Salmon Poetry.
Brian Donnelly teaches in the Department of English at University College Dublin.
Peter Kane Dufault is included in the *Norton Anthology of American Poetry*. He is the author of *New Things Come Into The World* (Lindisfarne Press, 1993), and

Looking In All Directions (Worple Press, 2000). His collected poems, *The Ponderable World*, covering more than five decades, is currently being assembled.

Joseph Fagan's poems have appeared in journals/magazines such as *Poetry Ireland Review*, *Acorn* , *Cúirt Journal*, and *Northwords* (Scotland), among others.

Janice Fitzpatrick-Simmons has published three collections: *Leaving America* (Lapwing, 1992), *Settler* (Salmon Poetry, 1995) and *Starting at Purgatory* (Salmon Poetry, 1999). She co-founded and is the current Director of The Poets' House/Teach na hÉigse, Falcarragh, Co. Donegal.

Matthew Fluharty poems have appeared in *Poetry Ireland Review*, *Black Mountain Review*, *THE SHOp*, *The New Writer*, *Avatar*, and elsewhere. Winner of two Academy of American Poets Awards, and the holder of a Master's Degree with Distinction from Poet's House/Lancaster University, he is current co-editor of *Breaking The Skin*.

John Fuller's collection *Now and for a Time* will be published by Chatto & Windus in April of this year. His *Collected Poems* were published in 1997, and will be reissued this year in paperback by Chatto & Windus. His most recent novel, *The Memoirs of Laetitia Horsepole, by Herself* (Chatto & Windus, 2001) will be reissued in paperback this year by Vintage.

Robert Greacen won the *Irish Times* Poetry Prize in 1995. His most recent publication is *Rooted In Ulster* (1991), a collection of essays on Northern Ireland.

Eamon Grennan's *Still Life With Waterfall* was published by Gallery Books, 2001.

Tom Halpin is a lecturer in the English Department at St. Patrick's College, Dublin.

Merrily Harpur co-founded and is the present Director of the Strokestown Poetry Festival.

Todd Hearon received a Robert Fitzgerald Translation Award in 2000 for his translations of Michael Hartnett's poems; other awards include the 2000 Paul Green Playwright's Prize. He is a previous contributor to *Poetry Ireland Review*.

Maria Hoey, a prize-winning short story writer, has just completed a first novel, *Saluting Magpies*.

Ben Howard's collection *Dark Pool* is forthcoming from Salmon Poetry in 2003. Salmon Poetry also published his verse novella *Midcentury* in 1997, while *The Pressed Melodeon: Essays on Modern Irish Writing* was published in 1996 by Story Line Press.

John Hughes has published three collections of poetry, his most recent being *The Devil Himself* (Gallery Books, 1996).

Gerry Hull's collection *Falling into Monaghan* was published by Salmon Poetry in 1999.

Hamish Ironside's poems are published in *P.N. Review*, *The Rialto* and *The Hegelian*, among others. The poem 'Some Vague Thing', included in this issue, was co-written with Oliver Sims.

Fred Johnston's most recent collection is *Being Anywhere – New & Selected Poems* (Lagan Press, 2002).

Rachel Kitzinger is Professor of Greek and Latin at Vassar College, New York.

Ann Leahy won the Patrick Kavanagh Award 2001 with *Teasing Roots from the Stem of a Geranium*. Publication credits include *Poetry Ireland Review*, *The Sunday Tribune*, *The New Writer's Collection*, and *Stand*. Her poems have been translated into Russian by poet Anatoly Kudryavitsky, and were published in February 2002 in a special Irish edition of *New Generation Literary Magazine* (Moscow), along with Michael Longley and Cathal Ó Searcaigh.

Mark Leeney is a member of Errigal Writers' group, and a prize-winner in a number of creative writing competitions. Last autumn he participated in the 'Poetry Ireland Introductions' readings.

Caroline Lynch won the Seán Dunne Memorial Poetry Competition in 1997.

Tom MacIntyre is a poet and playwright. His most recent collections are *Silenus na gCat* (Coiscéim, 1999), which won the Oireachtas prize for poetry, while *Stories of the Wandering Moon* was published by The Lilliput Press in 2000.

James J. McAuley's latest collection of poems is *Meditations, With Distractions: Poems 1989-1999* (University of Arkansas Press, 2001).

John McAuliffe is currently researching a study of Austin Clarke at Trinity College, Dublin. His poems and reviews have appeared in *Metre*, *The Irish Times*, *ROPES*, and *Southword*.

Hugh McFadden's verse has appeared in *Poetry Ireland Review* (Issue 1), *Aquarius*, *Broadsheet*, *The Cork Review*, *Cyphers*, and elsewhere. A collection, *Cities of Mirrors*, was published by Beaver Row Press. Another collection, *Elegies & Epiphanies* is forthcoming.

John McKernan's chapbook *Postcard From Dublin* was published recently by Dead Metaphor Press.

Michael Massey is co-ordinator of both Clogh Writers and K.A.R.A Writers.

Geraldine Mills' collection *Unearthing Your Own* was published last year by Bradshaw Books.

Noel Monahan's poetry collections include *Opposite Walls* (1991), *Snowfire* (1995) and *Curse of The Birds* (2000), all from Salmon Poetry. He is widely anthologised, most recently in *Awakenings*, a text on the New Leaving Certificate English syllabus. He is the winner in the Senior category of the inaugural SeaCat/Poetry Ireland National Poetry Competition.

Wendy Mooney's short stories have been published in *Stet*, and short-listed for various awards. 'Miss Delicious' (included in this issue) is her first published poem.

Patrick Moran's first collection of poems, *The Stubble Fields*, was published last year by Dedalus.

Gerry Murphy's collection *Torso Of An Ex-Girlfriend* is due out this year from Dedalus. *Rio De La Plata And All That* (not *Real De La Plata And All That*, as stated in recent issues of *Poetry Ireland Review*) was published by Dedalus in 1993.

Colette Nic Aodha has had poems published in *Feasta, Poetry Scotland, The Black Mountain Review, West 47, The Cúirt Journal, Comhar, An t-Ultach*, and *Lá*.

Eibhlín Nic Eochaidh is a member of the Knocknarea Writers Group. Her poems have appeared in *Poetry Ireland Review, College Green, Force 10* and *Women's Work IX*, and elsewhere. She won the Patrick Kavanagh Award in 1999.

Peggy O'Brien is the editor of the *Wake Forest Book of Irish Women's Poetry: 1967-2000* (Wake Forest University Press, 1999). Her poems and essays have appeared in major journals on both sides of the Atlantic.

Eugene O'Connell, a former editor of *Cork Literary Review*, has a new collection forthcoming in 2002.

John O'Donnell has had poems published in *The Irish Times, Sunday Tribune, Poetry Ireland Review, Stand*, and elsewhere. He won the Hennessy Award for Poetry in 1998, and the Listowel Writers' Week Prizes for Best Poem and Best Collection in 2001. His first collection is forthcoming.

Mary O'Donnell is a novelist and poet. Her third novel, *The Elysium Testament*, was published by Trident Press in 1999.

Ita O'Donovan has work published in various anthologies, including *Jumping The Bus Queue* and *Southword*. She is a member of Clifden Writers' Group.

Gréagóir Ó Dúill teaches at the Poets' House, Falcarragh. His *Rógha Dánta 1965-2001* was published last year by Cois Life / Coiscéim.

Leanne O'Sullivan attended Beara Community School, Beara, Co. Cork. She is the winner in the Secondary Schools category of the inaugural SeaCat/Poetry Ireland National Poetry Competition.

William Oxley's many publication credits include *Sparrow, The Formalist* (USA), *The Scotsman, New Statesman, Stand, The Spectator*, and *The Observer*. His most recent collection is *The Green Crayon Man* (Rockingham Press, 1997). His *Collected Longer Poems* was published in 1994 by Salzburg University Press.

Edward Power was previously published in *Poetry Ireland Review*.

Conall Quinn is a freelance writer and journalist.

Padraig Rooney's poems have appeared in *Poetry Review, International Quarterly, Prairie Schooner, Haiku World, Scanning the Century: The Penguin Book of the Twentieth Century in Poetry* (Penguin, 2000), and elsewhere.

Rosemarie Rowley has on three occasions won the Long Poem prize in the Scottish Open International competition. Her collections are *The Broken Pledge* (Martello, 1985), *The Sea of Affliction* (Rowan Tree Press, 1987), and a book-length poem *Flight Into Reality* (Rowan Tree Press, 1989, audiocassette 1996).

Joseph Sendry is Professor of English and Director of the Program in Comparative Literature at Catholic University in Washington, D.C.

John Sewell's most recent collection is *Bursting the Clouds* (Jonathan Cape, 1998)

John W. Sexton's collection of poems, *The Prince's Brief Career*, was published in 1996 by Cairn Mountain Publishing. His writing is previously published in *The Journal of Irish Literature, New Irish Writing, Poetry Ireland Review, Books Ireland, Cyphers, Incognito*, and elsewhere. His first novel, *The Johnny Coffin Diaries*, was published in 2001 by The O'Brien Press, and is based on *The Ivory Tower*, his children's radio show for RTÉ.

Gerard Smyth has contributed poetry to literary magazines in Ireland, Britain and North America. A new collection, *Daytime Sleeper: New and Selected Poems*, is forthcoming from Dedalus.

Eamonn Wall has published three collections of poetry, the most recent being *The Crosses* (Salmon Poetry, 2000).

Sabine Wichert has published two collections with Salmon, *Tin Drum Country (1995)* and *Sharing Darwin* (1999).

David Woelfel's recent publication credits include *The Stinging Fly, Books Ireland* and *Poetry Ireland Review*.

Mairíde Woods is a previous winner of the Francis MacManus award for short stories for radio, and the Hennessy Award for short stories. Her poems have been published in *Poetry Ireland Review, Women's Work, The Stinging Fly*, among other outlets.

Correction: Recent issues of *Poetry Ireland Review* have incorrectly attributed authorship of *Cape Clear: New and Selected Poems*, forthcoming from Salmon Poetry, to Peter Denman. Ted Deppe is in fact the author of *Cape Clear: New and Selected Poems*; Peter Denman, a former editor of *Poetry Ireland Review*, lectures in the English Department, NUI, Maynooth. His collection *The Poet's Manual* was published by Sotto Voce Press in 1991.

Books Received

Mention here does not preclude a review in a future issue.

Ed. by David Morley & Andy Brown, *Of Science*, Worple Press.
Ed. by John and Hilary Wakeman, *THE SHOp, Issue No. 7, Autumn/Winter 2001.*
Ed. by Brenda Miller, *Bellingham Review, Volume XXIV, No. 2, Issue #49, Fall 2001.*
Anne-Marie Fyfe, *Tickets from a Blank Window*, Rockingham Press.
Ed. by Phillis Levin, *The Penguin Book of the Sonnet*, Penguin Books.
Aidan McEoin, *In the Boat I Don't Yet Have: Collected Poems*, Singing Sands Publications.
Francis Harvey, *Making Space: New & Selected Poems*, The Dedalus Press.
Kevin Kiely, *Plainchant for a Sundering*, Lapwing.
Ed. by Daniel Veach, *Atlanta Review, Volume VIII, No. 1, Fall/Winter 2001.*
John Updike, *Americana and Other Poems*, Penguin Books.
Ed. by Tom Clyde, *HU, Issue 110, summer 2001.*
Billy Tinley, *Grace*, New Island Books.
Ed. by Sheila O'Hagan, *Cork Literary Review, Volume VIII.*
Ed. by Brian Henry & Andrew Zawacki, *Verse, Volume 18, Numbers 2 & 3, 2001.*
Ed. by Christopher Cahill, *The Recorder, Volume 14, No.2, Fall 2001.*
Dermot Healy, *The Reed Bed*, The Gallery Press.
Tom French, *Touching The Bones*, The Gallery Press.
Eiléan Ní Chuilleanáin, *The Girl Who Married The Reindeer*, The Gallery Press.
Dennis O'Driscoll, *Troubled Thoughts, Majestic Dreams: Selected Prose Writings*, The Gallery Press.
Ed. by David Pike, *Pulsar, December 2001, Edition 4/01 (28).*
Maurice Harmon, *Tales of Death and Other Poems*, Lapwing.
John McNamee, *The Trophy & New Writings*, Weaver Publications.
Anne Fitzgerald, *Swimming Lessons*, Stonebridge Publications.
Tony Curtis, *Heaven's Gate*, Seren.
Hilary Llewellyn-Williams, *Hummadruz*, Seren.
Christopher Daybell (ed. by Kate O'Shea), *The Man With the Crowded Eye: Selected Poems.*
Matt Simpson, *Getting There*, Liverpool University Press.
Marjorie Perloff, *21st-Century Modernism: The "New" Poetics*, Blackwell Manifestos, Blackwell Publishers.
Ed. by Oliver Marshall, *Wildeside Literary Magazine*, Issue 3, December 2001.
Ed. by Colin Blundell, *Blithe Spirit: Journal of The British Haiku Society*, Volume 11, Number 4, December 2001.
Linda Penkul, *The Windham Collection*, 1st Books Library.
Knute Skinner, *Greatest Hits: 1964-2000*, Pudding House Publications.
Patrick Conyngham, *Tulip In The Light*, Tuba Press.

Arklow Literary & Poetry Society 2001, *South of the Sugar Loaf.*
Pat Boran, *As The Hand, The Glove*, The Dedalus Press.
Patrick Moran, *The Stubble Field*s, The Dedalus Press.
The Small Press Guide 2002, Writers' Bookshop.
Robert Fraser, *The Chameleon Poet: A Life of George Barker*, Jonathan Cape.
Ed. by Patricia Oxley, *acumen 42, January 2002.*
Raymond Farina, *Exercices*, Maison de la Poésie D'amay.
Vikram Seth, *The Golden Gate*, Faber & Faber.
Richard Kell, *Collected Poems 1962-1993*, Lagan Press.
Ed. by David Hamilton, *The Iowa Review, Volume Thirty-One, Number Three 2001-2002.*
Ed. by Paul Perry, *Heartland: Writing from Longford.*
Ciaran O'Driscoll, *Moving On, Still There: News & Selected Poems*, Dedalus Press.
Ed. by Peter Forbes, *Poetry Review, Volume 91, Winter 2001/2002.*
Ed. by Niall McGrath, *The Black Mountain Review, Issue 5, Spring 2002.*
Ed. by Sally-Ann Murray, *Carapace 34.*
Ed. by Slakkie van der Schyffe, *Carapace 35.*
Phyllis McGuirk, *Marble Cherubs*, Riposte Books.
Ed. by Ernie Agnew & John Stevenson, *A Sense of Belonging* (East Side Arts).
John Stevenson, *Cowboys In Winter*, Lapwing.
Ed. by Pierre Dubrunquez, *poésie, No. 90/Décembre 2001.*
Ed. by David H. Lynn, *The Kenyon Review, Volume XXIV, Number 1, Winter 2002.*
Ed. by Robert Minhinnick, *Poetry Wales, Volume 37, Number 3, Winter 2002.*

Previous Editors of *Poetry Ireland Review*

John Jordan 1-8	Spring 1981 - Autumn 1983
Thomas McCarthy 9-12	Winter 1983 - Winter 1984
Conleth Ellis & Rita E. Kelly 13	Spring 1985
Terence Brown 14-17	Autumn 1985 - Autumn 1986
Ciarán Cosgrove 18/19	Spring 1987
Dennis O'Driscoll 20-21	Autumn 1987 - Spring 1988
John Ennis & Rory Brennan 22/23	Summer 1988
John Ennis 24-25	Winter 1988 - Spring 1989
Micheal O'Siadhail 26-29	Summer 1989 - Summer 1990
Máire Mhac an tSaoi 30-33	Autumn 1990 - Winter 1991
Peter Denman 34-37	Spring 1992 - Winter 1992
Pat Boran 38	Summer 1993
Seán Ó Cearnaigh 39	Autumn 1993
Pat Boran 40-42	Winter 1993 - Summer 1994
Chris Agee 43/44	Autumn/Winter 1994
Moya Cannon 45-48	Spring 1995 - Winter 1995
Liam Ó Muirthile 49	Spring 1996
Michael Longley 50	Summer 1996
Liam Ó Muirthile 51-52	Autumn 1996 - Spring 1997
Frank Ormsby 53-56	Summer 1997 - Spring 1998
Catherine Phil Mac Carthy 57-60	Summer 1998 - Spring 1999
Mark Roper 61-64	Summer 1999 - Spring 2000
Biddy Jenkinson 65-68	Summer 2000 - Spring 2001